PERSPECTIVES ON EDUCATION

PERSPECTIVES ON EDUCATION

By
Dr. Ismail Thamarasseri
Assistant Professor
Department of Education
Central University of Kashmir
Srinagar - 190 015
J&K (India)

DPH
DISCOVERY PUBLISHING HOUSE PVT. LTD.
INDIA

Published by:
Namit Wasan

DISCOVERY PUBLISHING HOUSE PVT. LTD.
4383/4B, Ansari Road, Darya Ganj
New Delhi-110 002 (India)
Phone : +91-11-23279245, 43596064-65
Fax : +91-11-23253475
E-mail: discoverypublishinghouse@gmail.com
namitwasan9@gmail.com
sales@discoverypublishinggroup.com
web : www.discoverypublishinggroup.com

***First Edition:* 2018**

ISBN: 978-93-5056-894-1

Perspectives on Education

Printed at:
Infinity Imaging Systems
Delhi

Preface

Education is the systematic process of improving learning, knowledge, skill and understanding about anything at school, college, university or other educational institutes which gives us an enlightening experience. Education is the most important factor which plays a great role in the development of an individual as well as a country. Now a day, it has become a vital factor for the future brightness of the new generations of any society. Education has been made fundamental right by the Government of India for all the children of age 6 to 14 years. Education influences lives of everyone in positive ways and teaches us to tackle any big or small problems in life. Even after a big awareness in the society towards the necessity of education for everyone, the percentage of education is still not same in different areas of the country. People living in the backward areas are not getting proper benefits of good education as they lack money and other resources. However, some new and effective strategies has been planned and implemented by the government to resolve the problems in such areas. Education improves the mental status and change the way of thinking of a person. It brings confidence and helps to convert the thinking into the action to go ahead and get success and experience.

Without education life becomes aimless and tough. So we should understand the importance of the education and its involvement in our daily lives. We should encourage the education in the backward areas by letting them know the benefits of education. Disabled people and poor people are equally required and have equal rights to get educated like rich and common people to get global development. Each of us should try our best to get educated at higher level as well as make the good education accessible for everyone globally particularly the poor and disabled people. Some people are completely uneducated and living very painful life because of the lack of training and skill development. Some people are formally educated but do not have enough skill to earn money for their daily routine just because of the lack of proper orientation. Thus we should try to have equal opportunities of good education system for everyone whether living in rich or poor regions. A country cannot grow and develop without the individual growth and development of its citizens. Thus the development of any country depends hugely on the education standard available to its citizens. A good education system must have common goals in every areas of country to provide a suitable and proper learning to its citizens.

For teachers who like to be facilitators and partners in the life of a student, this book offers valuable tools and insights. This book will introduce the readers to diverse thoughts on education. This book is a compilation of articles and research papers on various aspects of education developed by the author during last year's. Readers will identify, develop and apply a variety of thoughts congruent to their educational philosophy. The author hope that, this book is useful for those who interested in education in general and students of D.Ed., B.Ed., B.A. Education, M.A. Education and M.Ed. in particular. In this book, the author has drawn materials and data from various sources-such as, Government websites other URL's, standard works, journals, publications, reports, etc., the names of which have been duly incorporated in the References given to the end of units. The author express his gratitude to the writers, editors, publishers and other bodies of all these works. The author shall ever remain obliged to his teachers, parents, friends, colleagues, family members and students for their kind directions, guidance and assistance. The author takes this opportunity to express his sincere thanks to Prof. N.A. Nadeem, Prof. Nighat Basu, and all other staff members of the Central University of Kashmir for their valuable support. To them all, author offer his grateful thanks to M/s Discovery Publishing House Pvt. Ltd., New Delhi, who came forward willingly undertakes the publishing of this book.

Dr. Ismail Thamarasseri

Contents

1 Women's Movements in India

Introduction

The term "women's movement" does not refers to any single, unified movement, or entity. It is made of several movements based on the wide range of issues. It involves the using of different approaches at various points of time. These movements are focused towards the emancipation women. These movements aims at the reformulation of public life, the educational sphere, the work place, and the home in short, the aim is the total transformation of the society. Women's movements can be termed as conscious and collective movements that try to deal with the set of problems and need specific to women. These needs or problems are, in turn, created by the socio-cultural system that categorically puts them at the disadvantages in comparison to man. In general, resistance and protests against unjust structures of power and the institution of the patriarchy and patriarchal oppression of women begins with the oppression themselves. These oppressions are ever present and ubiquitous.

These forms of resistance are - manifest and latent - determine the method, strategies and techniques adopted by women to fight for their identity, dignity, self respect, and social justice. Sometimes women's movement contain the "zone of silent war" waged by women to gain control over men in everyday life. In the everyday life situation of women in the male-dominated world of most contemporary societies, the art of the resistance at the individual level, as well as organized collective movements coexist and even work simultaneously, through they may be conflicting practices and processes. The women studies of 1970s and 1980s shifted focus from the perspective of family, marriage, socialization, or social status to treat them as autonomous human beings. The emphasis today is on women's identity, consciousness, their subjectivity, and the bio-psychological foundations of their personality.

Women's Movements in India

The women's movements in India begin as the reform movements begin in India in the 19th century. The idea of the liberty, equality, and fraternity were being imbibed by the educated elites through the study of the English. Western liberalization was to extend to the women's question and translate in to awareness on the status of women. In India, the tradition of women's struggle and movements against patriarchal institution of gender injustice has been weak when compared to the women's movements of the western and the European societies. In fact the women's movements in India are rather slow in emerging. The women's movements in India can be seen as forming three waves. The first wave can be seen during the national movements, when there is a mass mobilization of women's for the participation in national movements. Thereafter, for over a decade there was a lull in political activities by women. The late 1960s saw resurgence in women's in political activities and can be called as the second wave. In the late 1970s, the third wave of the women's movements emerges, which focuses on the women's empowerment.

Challenges to Gender Equality

Challenges to gender equality occur in many ways. Some of the Issues are:

- **Education:** Men tend to have higher educational attain-ments, though in many societies in the world this gap is rapidly closing.
- **Wages and Employment:** Men occupying the same jobs as women tend to be paid more, promoted more frequently, and receive more recognition for their accomplishments.
- **Healthcare:** In some countries men have more access to and receive better healthcare than women.
- **Violence and Exploitation:** Women are subjected to violence and exploitation at greater rates than men.
- **Social Inequality:** Women still perform the majority of domestic duties like housework and childcare.

Pre-independence Women's Movements in India

There have been the acts of resistance in India from since the immemorial times like Rezia Sultan, Rani Lakhshmibai of Jhansi, have questioned and went against the existing system. Women throughout history made efforts to break bonds from the various castes they have to face by virtue of their birth. Many women joined the *Bhakti Movement*. The saints stood for the equal rights for both men and women. Some of the women become the leading poets such as Mira bai, Janaki etc.

The Social Reform Movements and Women

The social reformers believe in the principle of individual liberty, freedom and equality of human beings irrespective of their caste, sex, colour, race and religion. They attacked a no of traditional, authoritarian, and hierarchical social institutions and launched social reform movement to liberate Indian women from their shackles. Though many of the reformers were mainly men, the reform movement aimed at improving the status of Indian women.

- **Raja Ram Mohan Roy:** Raja Ram Mohan Roy was one of the great reformers of India. He was concerned about the evil customs planning in Indian society. These includes *sati*, female infanticide, polygamy, infant marriage, *Purdha* system, absence of education among the women etc. Raja Ram arguments and anti-sati activities led Lord William Bentinck to legislate for the prohibition of sati, which result in the passing of the prohibition of sati Act in 1929.
- **Ishwer Chandra Vidyasagar:** He was another social reformer who sought to improve the condition of the widows by legalizing widow remarriage. So he set his life as the example for the others to follow, he took a pledge that he would allow his daughter to study and marry all his daughters after they were 16 years of age he was also against the prevalent system of polygamy.
- **Justice Mahadev Govind Ranade:** He play an instrumental role in laying the down the foundation of an all Indian organization to carry the struggle for social reform. He took the steps towards the education of women and widow remarriage.
- **The Gujrat Vernacular Society:** This social institution is to be established in 1848, associated with the decrease in large-scale illiteracy, superstitious belief and women education in large.
- **The Deccan Education Society:** The society was formed in 1884. The society started girl school and encourage education of women in Maharashtra.
- **The Ramakrishana Mission:** The Ramakrishna was established in 1897. It sets up homes for widows and school for girls.
- **The Arya Samaj:** It lays emphasis on the women education.

Participation of Women in National Struggle

Sarojini Naidu was one of the forerunners of women participation in the national movement. She uses her poetry to rejuvenate the spirit of independence. In 1920 she joined the non-cooperation movement. In 1930 M.K. Gandhi launched the civil disobedience movement she led the movement with other congress member. After the Jalianwala bagh incident women become politically conscious. As a result women become the part of the struggle movement.

Post-Independence Women Movements in India

There is a distinction between the pre- independence movement and the post independence women's movements in India. The-independence movement were essentially about social reforms and is initiated by man. In comparison, the post independence movement demand gender equality, questioned gender based division of labour and highlighted the oppressive nature of the existing patriarchal structures in the euphoria of the post independence, it was believed that the women's status would dramatically increase with the other marginalized sections of the society. After the India gained the independence from British rule in 1947, it was the congress party that came in power and formed the government. The government made certain attempts to fulfil the promises it had made to the women during the pre-independence period and even after independence. While framing the constitution of India, it includes the very aspects of the equality of men and women in all the sphere of life.

- Article 14: Equality before the law or the equal protection of the law with in the territory of India.
- Article 15: State shall not discriminate against any citizen on the grounds of religion, race, sex, place of birth, or any of them.
- Article 15 (A): Nothing in the article shall prevent the state from making any special provision for women and children."
- Article 16: Equal opportunities to all the citizens related to employment and the appointment in any office under the state.

The constitutional provisions promise of equality did not resolved the question of gender inequality. Especially in India which is so diverse. Comprise of different cultures and religions. The challenge to address inequality within women in India remain till days. The issues of women's started to be communalized and the various women's organizations and the feminist did not know how to deal with problem of the women of different religion. Then a period started when the NGOs has started which deals with issue of women's. In 1972 an organization was formed by the initiative of *Elabhat* called as self employed women's association (SAWA) whose aim is at improving the working condition of the women through a process of training, technical aid, legal, literacy, collective bargaining, and to teach the value of the honesty, dignity, simplicity. After that women's stated participating in the increased no in the Naxalbari movement in west Bengal Naxilite movement in Andhra Pradesh, the Navnirman Youth Movement in Gujarat, and the Chipko movement. The progressive organization of women came in to existence.

Contemporary Women's Movements in India

The contemporary women's movements in India were initiated by the Declaration of UN year of the women in 1975. This report directly attacked the myth that women's in post independent India were progressing. It revealed that a majority of the women in India were suffering from poverty, illiteracy, and ill-health, as well as the discrimination in both the domestic and public sphere, these results in the agitation and campaigns against the worst manifestation of sexism patriarchy by the middle-class women. The report of the committee on the status of women proves to by turning point in the path of contemporary women's movements in India. The report made the following recommendation:

- Equality not merely for justice but for deployment;
- Force should be on economic empowerment of women;
- Child bearing should be shared as a social responsibility;
- Recognition of household works as national productivity;
- Marriage and motherhood should not be disability;
- Emancipation of women should be linked to social emancipation; and
- Special temporary measures for de facto equality.

The year 1975, saw the development of a number of feminist activities in various parts of the country, especially in Maharashtra. This is seen as an in direct result of UN's declaration of 1975, as the international women year. On 8th, March 1975 the international women day was celebrated for the first time by both parties and autonomous organization in Maharashtra. In 1975, the Prime Minister Indira Gandhi declared a state emergency throughout the country. This interrupted the development of the women movement in India. In 1977, emergency was lifted; this led to the revival of women's movement that has been brought to a standstill by the declaration of emergency. Women's group was formed in most parts of the country. The 1980s witnessed a transformation of the women's movements. Organizations increased their focus from one or two issues to deal with holistic issue there were three different streams of feminist of orientations:

- The Liberal Stream focuses on demanding reforms in those aspects of the polity which specially affect women.
- The Leftist Stream situates oppression of women within a holistic analysis of the general structure of oppression and calls for a coming together of specific movements for social change in order to effect the revolutionary transformation of society.
- The Radical feminists concentrate on defining the development of feminity and masculinity in society as fundamental polarities, and experimented with reclaiming traditional sources of women's strength, creativity, and so on.

The Movement against Dowry

Death of young married women within the family had long been treated as "accidental" and recorded as "suicides". The women's movement drew the link between demands for dowry and the deaths. They demanded re-categorization of such deaths as "Murder' and not "Suicide". The first campaign of the contemporary feminist movement was against dowry. Dowry is the sum of all the money as well as other items such as jewellery, cars, furniture, and house etc. given by the bride's family to the groom and his family. After the emergency was lifted in 1977, a new movement against dowry started in Delhi. This movement focused upon the violence inflicted upon women for dowry, including bride burning and abetment to suicide.

The government passed a law against dowry and related crimes in 1980. This law declared/treated abetment to suicide arising from dowry demands as a special crime. It made a police investigation into the death of any woman within five years of marriage mandatory. In 1985, the Supreme Court upheld the verdict, but converted the verdict from death sentence to life imprisonment. In the same year, the Criminal law (Second Amendment) Act was passed. This made cruelty to a wife a cognizable, non billable offence, punishable by up to three years imprisonment and fine. Section 1741 of the Criminal Procedure Code, which makes a post-mortem of the body of woman who dies within seven years of marriage compulsory.

The Movement against the Rape

There was the movement against the government officials, police, land lords in the rural and the urban areas in India. This issue gained the prominence because of the incident of the Ramzana Bee in Hyderabad. Ramzana bee was raped by the several police men. Her husband, a rickshaw puller was murdered when he protested against his wife's rape. As reaction; thousand of the peoples went to the police station, laid the man's dead body in the station veranda; set up roadblocks, stoned the buildings and set fire to some of the vehicles. The army was called in, and the demonstration and protests were quieted only after the state government was dismissed and a commission was set up to look the case of the rape and murder. There are the number of the cases that trigger these feminists to stand against these social evils, they started protest and demonstration against these cases.

In 1980 local policeman in Maharashtra raped a 16 year old girl. The decision goes against the girl. This was the first time when the feminist group campaign against this decision. In 1980 Maya Tyagi case where we see the country wide demonstrations protest. The recent case 16 December, 2012 (India's Daughter) made the government to think about the law's related the rape, physical abuse and the crime related to the women's. On seen the wide protest and demonstration from all the corners of the country for the justice of the victim on the fast track, Justice Verma Committee was setup to solve the case, and all the six culprits were arrested but this put a big question mark on our laws related to these cases. An amendment has been passed the 7 years of punishment is to be replaced by the life impressments or shall be hanged.

REFERENCES

1. Mukhopadhyaya, A. *Social Movements in India.*
2. Ghanshyam, S. *Social Movements in India.*
3. The Editors of Salem Press. *Theories of Social Movement.*

2 Understanding the Teachers Role in Preventing Gender-based Violence

Introduction

Gender-based violence (GBV) is violence involving men and women, in which the female is usually the victim; and which is derived from unequal power relationships between men and women. Violence is directed specifically against a woman because she is a woman, or affects women disproportionately. It includes, but is not limited to, physical, sexual, and psychological harm. It includes that violence which is perpetuated or ignored by the state. (UNFPA, 1998). As most types of GBV are carried out under the cover of culture and tradition, and are deeply rooted in the community, addressing this issue requires engagement of the community as a whole. Education is one of the powerful tool against GBV. Educated women are less likely to have undesired life outcomes. Providing girls with educational opportunities improves their status in the community. We can help by encouraging parents to send their daughters to school and by encouraging girls to go to school and to continue with their schooling. Girls and women often lack information on reproductive health issues, but education gives them necessary knowledge. We can also involve women as members and leaders of community-based health committees. Involving boys and men in fighting GBV will have a lasting effect. As we know, it is usually boys and men who impose violence on girls and women, so any effort to abolish GBV without their engagement will not be successful. Teachers can help students to understand that boys and girls are different but equal and everyone deserves equal respect. Teachers can use various methods to mobilise the community and improve their awareness and behaviour. Community conversation is a good medium to fight GBV. As an influential professional, teacher can tell to student and community members of the advantages of improving women's health by fighting GBV and to explain that policy makers and religious leaders want all individuals to have full and equal rights.

GBV encompasses a range of physical, sexual, and psychological violence that disproportionately affects women and girls (IGWG/USAID, 2008). Violence against women is a major problem that negatively affects the reproductive health of women and girls. "Each year as many as 40 million children under 15 years old experience some form of violence. Many of them are girls, and many live in Africa" (African Child Policy Forum, 2006). Although the global community has focused greater attention on GBV in recent years, levels of violence against women remain unchanged (UN General Assembly, 2006). Eliminating GBV is a "profoundly political challenge, because it necessitates challenging the unequal social, political, and economic power of men and women and the ways in which this inequality is perpetuated through institutions at all levels of society" (Ward, 2005).

Various Forms of GBV include battering, intimate partner violence, (including marital rape, sexual violence, and dowry-related violence), female infanticide, foeticide, sexual abuse of female children in the household, honour crimes, early marriage, forced marriage, female genital cutting and other traditional practices harmful to women, sexual harassment in the workplace and educational institutions, commercial sexual exploitation, trafficking of girls and women, and violence perpetrated against domestic workers (USAID, 2009). Violence against women is a very common problem in all over the world and can happen to any woman in any culture. It is a violation of human rights. It is also a public health problem, though it has not been given due considerations as a public health problem. It affects every aspect of the woman's life and has many complex sexual and reproductive health consequences. In this session, you will learn about the consequences of the major forms of violence against women. You will also learn how you can help girls and women who are victims of violence. Sex is the biological characteristic that defines humans as female or male, while gender refers to socially and culturally defined roles for males and females. Gender refers to socially and culturally defined roles for males and females. These roles are learned over time, can change from time to time, and vary widely within and between cultures. Gender is not only about girls/women. However, the traditionally defined gender roles disadvantage girls and women.

Gender-based violence (GBV) is any form of deliberate physical, psychological or sexual harm, or threat of harm, directed against a person on the basis of their gender. Although gender-based violence is not exclusively directed against females, they do suffer from it the most, which is why the focus of this study session is on women and girls. GBV is a violation of fundamental human rights. Violence against girls and women prevents them from enjoying their rights. Fundamental human rights to which everyone is entitled without distinction based on race, sex, language, religion, political or other opinions.

- Everyone has the right to life, liberty and security of person.
- No one shall be subjected to torture or to cruel, inhuman or degrading treatment or punishment.
- Everyone has the right to a standard of living adequate for health and wellbeing.
- Everyone has the right to social security and personal development.
- Everyone has the right to education.
- Everyone has the right to freedom of opinion and expression.

When violence occurs against girls and women, it is usually committed by boys or men. Violence against women stems from the unequal power relations between men and women. A person with more power has many choices, while a person with less power has few choices. There are many types of power, such as economic power (control or access to money and other resources) and physical power (strength or weapons). The person with less power is vulnerable in many ways. Women have less power than men and as a consequence are more vulnerable to violence. The most common form of violence is the violence against girls and women at the household level. In most communities, this GBV is accepted as normal behaviour and there is little awareness of GBV as an issue that needs attention. It is not treated as a serious crime but as a private matter even though it has serious consequences for girls and women. Violence against women and girls takes place throughout their lives, starting in infancy and continuing to old age. Examples include the preference for a male child, trafficking for labour and sexual abuse, rape, wife beating, food restriction, early marriage, abduction, female genital mutilation and wife inheritance. There are various factors that make girls and women vulnerable to acts of violence, such as:

- They lack power.
- They have low status.
- They are often less educated.
- They are often poor and economically dependent on men and this inequality places them in a situation where they are easily abused.
- Cultural beliefs and values reinforce rigid gender roles and the low status of women. Most of the violence against girls and women is perpetrated under the cover of culture.
- Limited awareness (among both females and males) about the rights of girls and women.
- Boys and men commonly drink alcohol and use other mind-altering substances which impair judgement and/or make them violent.

Types of gender-based violence

Physical	Mental	Sexual
Beating	Insulting	Harassment (any type of unwanted sexual attention)
Biting	Yelling	Touching sexual parts of the girl's/woman's body
Kicking	Recalling past mistakes	Touching in a sexual manner against the will of the girl/woman (e.g. kissing, grabbing, fondling)
Restraining	Constant criticism	Rape (forced sexual intercourse)
Pulling hair	Expressing negative expectations	Use of a weapon to force into a sexual act
Choking	Humiliation	Forced prostitution
Throwing objects	Denying opportunities	Sexual trafficking
Sing weapons	Discriminating	

Although same-sex physical violence (even including stabbing) can be common among adolescents, the unequal power relationship results in most physical violence being directed at girls by boys. Psychological GBV can be hidden, but you might uncover it if you ask some questions, for example, you could ask a very under-confident young girl whether she is receiving a lot of criticism from her family for being a girl. Sexual violence includes a wide variety of undesired sexual acts, ranging from sexual harassment, which includes unpleasant sexual comments or physical gestures, to sexual abuse, which is any type of unwanted sexual contact and includes all forms of sexual coercion (emotional, physical, and economic) against an individual. Rape is defined as having sex with a woman or girl without her consent or with consent obtained under threat, force, intimidation, fear of bodily harm or misrepresentation. Many adolescents are forced to have sexual relations with men or boys they know and are assaulted if they refuse to have sex. If a boyfriend forces his girlfriend to have sex against her will this is called date rape while acquaintance rape is committed by someone who is known to the girl, such as a neighbour, teacher, religious leader, family friend or relative. But sometimes a stranger commits an act of sexual violence.

Consequences of Gender-based Violence (GBV)

GBV that involves physical violence could lead to a physical injury, from a simple wound to loss of body parts and even death. GBV also causes psychological trauma such as fear, anxiety, self-blame, depression and suicidal thoughts. It is not usually visible (unlike physical trauma) but girls/women suffer a great deal from it and the effects can be longer-lasting than a physical injury and affect behaviour and interpersonal relationships. For example, women who are sexually abused during their childhood tend to feel guilty about the abuse. They develop negative feelings about themselves and lose self-esteem. These bad feelings about themselves often causes them to engage in high-risk behaviours and practices. This makes them more vulnerable to Sexually Transmitted Infections (STIs) including HIV, unwanted pregnancies and infertility. GBV-related Health Consequences for Adolescence tabulated below.

Fatal Outcomes	Nonfatal Outcomes		
	Physical	Sexual and Reproductive	Psychological and Behavioural
• Femicide	• Fractures	• Sexually transmitted infections, including HIV	• Depression and anxiety
• Suicide	• Chronic pain syndromes	• Unintended pregnancy	• Eating and sleep disorders
• AIDS-related mortality	• Fibromyalgia	• Pregnancy complications	• Drug and alcohol abuse
• Maternal mortality	• Permanent disability	• Traumatic gynecologic	• Poor self-esteem
	• Gastro-intestinal disorders	• Fistula • Abortion complications	• Post-traumatic stress disorder • Self-harm

Note: Adapted from Heise *et al.*, 1999.

Barriers to Reporting Sexual Violence

Reasons for not reporting GBV include:

- **Fear of stigma and discrimination:** Someone who has been raped may be seen by others as unclean. She will be blamed for what has happened to her and may experience discrimination.
- **Blame:** Society expects girls and women to be able to avoid sexual violence including rape. If any form of sexual violence occurs, society often blames the woman for the way she behaves and dresses, saying that the rape is her fault because she has provoked sexual desires in boys and men.
- **Fear of disbelief:** Many girls do not think anyone will believe them, particularly if they have been abused by someone they know. For this reason, many people who have experienced sexual violence, including children, remain silent.
- **Fear of revenge:** Many girls and women who are raped are intimidated by their attacker, who threatens that he and his family and friends will cause her further harm if she makes a police report. They may even make death threats.

- **Ineffective policing:** Even when young women who have been raped do report the case to the police they may not achieve much. They are not often protected by the police and if the wrong doer is not imprisoned they may be in greater danger than before.
- **Health workers' attitudes:** People who have experienced sexual violence can recover from the trauma if they find someone who will acknowledge their experience and provide support. One way they could heal is through hearing encouraging words from healthcare providers. However, health workers are not usually understanding and supportive when someone who has been raped seeks care from health facilities. They often tend to be judgemental. This is why many girls who experience GBV will seek practical help for health issues but will not talk about the violence that has caused them to attend at the health post.

Empowering Women through Education

"Education is one of the most important means of empowering women with the knowledge, skills and self-confidence necessary to participate fully in the development process." (ICPD Programme of Action). Education is important for everyone, but it is especially significant for girls and women. This is true not only because education is an entry point to other opportunities, but also because the educational achievements of women can have ripple effects within the family and across generations. Investing in girls' education is one of the most effective ways to reduce poverty. Investments in secondary school education for girls yields especially high dividends. Girls who have been educated are likely to marry later and to have smaller and healthier families. Educated women can recognize the importance of health care and know how to seek it for themselves and their children. Education helps girls and women to know their rights and to gain confidence to claim them. However, women's literacy rates are significantly lower than men's in most developing countries.

Education has far-reaching Effects

The education of parents is linked to their children's educational attainment, and the mother's education is usually more influential than the father's. An educated mother's greater influence in household negotiations may allow her to secure more resources for her children. Educated mothers are more likely to be in the labour force, allowing them to pay some of the costs of schooling, and may be more aware of returns to schooling. And educated mothers, averaging fewer children, can concentrate more attention on each child. Besides having fewer children, mothers with schooling are less likely to have mistimed or unintended births. This has implications for schooling, because poor parents often must choose which of their children to educate.

Constitutional Provisions and Current debates on Women Education

The Constitution of India not only grants to women but also empowers the State to adopt measures of positive discrimination in favour of women for neutralizing the cumulative socio-economic, education and political disadvantages faced by them. Fundamental Rights, among others, ensures equality before the law, equal protection of law, prohibits discrimination against any citizen on grounds of religion, race, caste, sex or place of birth, and guarantees equality of opportunity to all citizens in matters relating to employment. Articles 14, 15, 15(3), 16, 39(a), 39(b), 39(c) and 42 of the Indian constitution are of specific importance in this regard.

Role of Women Leaders in Education of Women

Women education in India plays key role in the overall development of the country. It not only helps in the development of half of the human resources, but in improving the quality of life at home and outside. An educated woman not only tends to promote education of their girl children, but also can provide better guidance to all their children. Moreover educated women can also help in the reduction of infant mortality rate and growth of the population. Gender discrimination still persists in India and lot more needs to be done in the field of women's education in India. Women education is most important than men education. Not only in India all over the world women education is neglected in earlier. Everybody remembered what had happened in the early days. Indian social reformers had began the devote attention to the cause of woman's emancipation. Most of the social reformers like Savitri bai Phule, Panditha Rama Bhai, Sarojini Naidu, Mother Theresa, Sarojini Nalini Dutt, Sarojini Devi Bhattacharyya, and some other propagated the impotence women Education. The social reformers tried to use education more ameliorate the position of women socially; they were able to awaken the consciousness of the nation to the evils of child marriage, sati, and polygamy, enforced widowhood, dowry system etc. The lack of education means the lack of self-reliance, self confidence for which women are not able to come out of their problems. Reform movements gained momentum most proponents of women's education, despite varied motivations, seemed to believe in education for enlightened motherhood and took a narrow, domestic perspective of the social roles of women. Women leaders are played key in the improvement of the women education and women empowerment.

School-related Gender-based Violence is Preventing the Achievement of Quality Education for All

The number of years a person spends in school has been shown to have a positive correlation with a decrease in both future victimisation and perpetration of physical and sexual violence. Education increases women's employment opportunities and socio-economic status. The empowerment of women reduces the unequal power relationship between women and men which has been identified as the root cause of GBV. However the level of education is a very blunt measurement, and if not properly addressed, schools can instead turn into reproducers of harmful societal norms and practices and become unsafe. It is therefore necessary for schools and other educational institutions to apply strategies to prevent and respond to violence. Here, teachers play a key role and the introduction of gender-responsive pedagogy in the education process, as does sexuality education in the school curricula. This can help unlock the potential of schools as sites for empowerment of girls and boys and for the prevention of GBV.

Evidence indicates that School-Related Gender-Based Violence (SRGBV) affects millions of children and adolescents worldwide. It is one of the worst manifestations of gender discrimination and violates a wide range of children's rights. Education is critical in empowering and transforming the lives of young people, especially girls, yet widespread gender-based violence in and around schools seriously undermines the achievement of quality, inclusive and equitable education for all children. The 2006 UN World Report on Violence Against Children identified violence again children – including in school settings – as a global phenomenon. Yet almost a decade later we still do not know the full scale and impact of gender-based violence in schools. Much research on violence against children in schools has neglected to explore the role of gender, yet most forms of school violence are deeply rooted in unequal gender relations, gendered social norms and discriminatory practices.

Moreover, while the increasing recognition of SRGBV is a positive trend, rarely has this been translated into effective policies that demonstrate a reduction in prevalence (Parkes, 2015). If we are to "build and upgrade education facilities that are child, disability and gender sensitive and provide safe, non-violent, inclusive and effective learning environments for all" – a proposed post-2015 target in education - we need better information and more evidence on SRGBV. We need to understand the nature and extent of the problem worldwide. We need to know why it happens and with what consequences. We need robust data to develop strategies and evaluate their success in reducing SRGBV.

Conclusion

A gender responsive school is one where the academic, social and physical environment and its surrounding community take into account the specific needs of both girls and boys. The academic delivery, including teaching methodologies, teaching and learning materials, classroom interaction and management of academic processes, should be gender responsive. In the school level, school administration, teachers and other staffs can play a role in addressing SRGBV. School code of conduct, responsive with gender based violence including a discussion of codes of conduct in teacher training curricula is also important for addressing SRGBV. It is also necessary to incorporate gender, rights and violence prevention contents in the curriculum of schools and universities (Bott *et al.*, 2004). Likewise, some countries approached to train students, teacher, community leaders and community to prevent and respond to school-related gender violence in their communities (Mlamleli *et al.*, 2001). To promote the enrolment rate of females in schools, some programs have practiced by establishing single sex schools, hiring more female teachers, building separate latrines or canteens for girls, reducing the distance that girls must travel to receive an education, and/or providing in-service gender sensitivity training to educators and administrators (UNICEF, 2004). Hence, several developed countries have adopted different strategies and programs to cope with the violent situations in academic arena. For instance, the roots of empathy program, public awareness program, living values program and white ribbon campaign, raising voices programs are implemented in academic settings to reduce the violent activities in schools and to make learning environment more equitable. Some of these programs are implemented in public spheres and some are implemented solely in the schools and curriculum as well. But we have big gap between the practices and existing phenomena of gender based violence in our schools due to the lack of research.

REFERENCES

1. *Gender-Based Violence.*, retrieved from http://www.open.edu/openlearnworks/mod/oucontent/view.php?id=67
2. Heise, L., M. Ellsberg, and M. Gottemoeller. 1999. "Ending Violence against Women." *Population Reports* XXVII (Series L, Number 11). Available at: www.infoforhealth.org/pr/l11/violence.pdf (accessed October 14, 2009).
3. *Understanding Violent Behaviour In Children and Adolescents.*, American Academy of Child and Adolescent Psychiatry., retrieved from http://www.aacap.org
4. Thamarasseri, Ismail. (2015). *Adolescence Education.* New Delhi: Dominant Publishers & Distributors (P) Ltd.
5. *Gender-Based Violence and Education.*, retrieved on 08-11-2016 from http://www.sida.se/contentassets/3a820dbd152f4fca98bacde8a8101e15/genderbased-violence-and-education.pdf
6. *School-related gender-based violence is preventing the achievement of quality education for all.*, retrieved on 08-11-2016 from http://www.ungei.org/srgbv/files/232107E.pdf
7. Poudel, T.N. Gender and Violence in School: Current Phenomena and Copping Strategies. *The SIJ Transactions on Industrial, Financial & Business Management* (IFBM), Vol. 2, No. 3, May 2014., retrieved on 08-11-2016 from http://www.thesij.com/papers/IFBM/2014/May/IFBM-0203240401.pdf

3

Children's Rights Education

Introduction

Children's rights are the human rights of children with particular attention to the rights of special protection and care to minors, including their right to association with both parents, human identity as well as the basic needs for food, universal state-paid education, health care and criminal laws appropriate for the age and development of the child, equal protection of the child's civil rights, and freedom from discrimination on the basis of the child's race, gender, sexual orientation, gender identity, national origin, religion, disability, colour, ethnicity, or other characteristics. Interpretations of children's rights range from allowing children the capacity for autonomous action to the enforcement of children being physically, mentally and emotionally free from abuse. Children's rights education is the teaching and practice of children's rights in schools and educational institutions. When fully implemented, a children's rights education program consists of both a curriculum to teach children their human rights, and framework to operate the school in a manner that respects children's rights.

Children's human rights education refers to education and educational practices in schools and educational institutions that are consistent with the United Nations Convention on the Rights of the Child. It is a form of education that takes seriously the view that children are bearers of human rights, that children are citizens in their own right, that schools and educational institutions are learning communities where children learn (or fail to learn) the values and practices of human rights and citizenship, and that educating children about their own basic human rights is a legal obligation of the UN Convention on the Rights of the Child. Children's rights education is education where the rights of the child, as described in the Convention, is taught and practiced in individual classrooms. But in its most developed form, children's rights are taught and practiced in a systematic and comprehensive way across grade levels, across the school, and across school districts. With full-blown children's rights education, children's rights are not simply an addition to a particular subject or classroom. Rather, the rights of the child are incorporated into the school curricula, teaching practices, and teaching materials across subjects and grade levels and are the centrepiece of school mission statements, behaviour codes, and school policies and practices.

A child is any human being below the age of eighteen years, unless under the law applicable to the child, majority is attained earlier. A child is a person, not a sub person. The term "child" often, but does not necessarily, mean minor, but can include adult children as well as adult non-dependent children. There are no definitions of other terms used to describe young people such as "adolescents", "teenagers," or "youth" in international law, but the children's rights movement is considered distinct from the youth rights movement. The field of children's rights spans the fields of law, politics, religion, and morality. As minors by law children do not have autonomy or the right to make decisions on their own for themselves in any known jurisdiction of the world. Instead their adult caregivers, including parents, social workers, teachers, youth workers, and others, are vested with that authority, depending on the circumstances. Some believe that this state of affairs gives children insufficient control over their own lives and causes them to be vulnerable. Structures such as government policy have been held by some commentators to mask the ways adults' abuse and exploit children, resulting in child poverty, lack of educational opportunities, and child labour. On this view, children are to be regarded as a minority group towards whom society needs to reconsider the way it behaves. Researchers have identified children as needing to be recognized as participants in society whose rights and responsibilities need to be recognized at all ages.

Historic Definitions of Children's Rights

Consensus on defining children's rights has become clearer in the last fifty years. The notion of children's rights is still not well defined, with at least one proposing that there is no singularly accepted definition or theory of the rights held by children. Children's rights law is defined as the point where the law intersects with a child's life. That includes juvenile delinquency, due process for children involved in the criminal justice system, appropriate representation, and effective rehabilitative services; care and protection for children in state care; ensuring education for all children regardless of their race, gender, sexual orientation, gender identity, national origin, religion, disability, colour, ethnicity, or other characteristics, and; health care and advocacy.

Types of Child Rights

Children's rights are defined in numerous ways, including a wide spectrum of civil, cultural, economic, social and political rights. Rights tend to be of two general types: those advocating for children as autonomous persons under the law and those placing a claim on society for protection from harms perpetrated on children because of their dependency. These have been labelled as the right of empowerment and as the right to protection. Child Rights Information Network (CRIN) categorizes child rights into following groups.

- Provision: Children have the right to an adequate standard of living, health care, education and services, and to play and recreation. These include a balanced diet, a bed to sleep in, and access to schooling.
- Protection: Children have the right to protection from abuse, neglect, exploitation and discrimination. This includes the right to safe places for children to play; constructive child rearing behaviour, and acknowledgment of the evolving capacities of children.
- Participation: Children have the right to participate in communities and have programs and services for themselves. This includes children's involvement in libraries and community programs, youth voice activities, and involving children as decision-makers.
- Economic, social and cultural rights, related to the conditions necessary to meet basic human needs such as food, shelter, education, health care, and gainful employment. Included are rights to education, adequate housing, food, water, the highest attainable standard of health, the right to work and rights at work, as well as the cultural rights of minorities and indigenous peoples.
- Environmental, cultural and developmental rights, which are sometimes called "third generation rights," and including the right to live in safe and healthy environments and that groups of people have the right to cultural, political, and economic development.

Amnesty International openly advocates four particular children's rights, including the end to juvenile incarceration without parole, an end to the recruitment of military use of children, ending the death penalty for people under 21, and raising awareness of human rights in the classroom. Human Rights Watch, an international advocacy organization, includes child labour, juvenile justice, orphans and abandoned children, refugees, street children and corporal punishment. The following rights "allow children to grow up healthy and free":

- Freedom of speech
- Freedom of thought
- Freedom from fear
- Freedom of choice and the right to make decisions
- Ownership over one's body

Other issues affecting children's rights include the military use of children, sale of children, child prostitution and child pornography.

Difference between Children's Rights and Youth Rights

In the majority of jurisdictions, for instance, children are not allowed to vote, to marry, to buy alcohol, to have sex, or to engage in paid employment. Within the youth rights movement, it is believed that the key difference between children's rights and youth rights is that children's rights supporters generally advocate the establishment and enforcement of protection for children and youths, while youth rights (a far smaller movement) generally advocates the expansion of freedom for children and/ or youths and of rights such as suffrage.

Common Sense Parenting

Parents affect the lives of children in a unique way, and as such their role in children's rights has to be distinguished in a particular way. Particular issues in the child-parent relationship include child neglect, child abuse, freedom of choice, corporal punishment and child custody. There have been theories offered that provide parents with rights-based practices that resolve the tension between "common sense parenting" and children's rights. The issue is particularly relevant in legal proceedings that affect the potential emancipation of minors and in cases where children sue their parents. A child's rights to a relationship with both their parents are increasingly recognized as an important factor for determining the best interests of the child in divorce and child custody proceedings. Some governments have enacted laws creating a rebuttable presumption that shared parenting is in the best interests of children.

Convention on the Rights of the Child (CRC)

The Universal Declaration of Human Rights is seen as a basis for all international legal standards for children's rights today. There are several conventions and laws that address children's rights around the world. A number of current and historical documents affect those rights, including the 1923 Declaration of the Rights of the Child, drafted by Eglantyne Jebb and her sister Dorothy Buxton in London, England in 1919, endorsed by the League of Nations and adopted by the United Nations in 1946. It later served as the basis for the Convention on the Rights of the Child. The United Nations' 1989 Convention on the Rights of the Child, or CRC, is the first legally binding international instrument to incorporate the full range of human rights-civil, cultural, economic, political and social rights. Its implementation is monitored by the Committee on the Rights of the Child. National governments that ratify it commit themselves to protecting and ensuring children's rights, and agree to hold themselves accountable for this commitment before the international community. The CRC is the most widely ratified human rights treaty with 190 ratifications.

Vienna Declaration and Programme of Action

Vienna Declaration and Programme of Action urges at Section II para 47, all nations to undertake measures to the maximum extent of their available resources, with the support of international cooperation, to achieve the goals in the World Summit Plan of Action. And calls on States to integrate the Convention on the Rights of the Child into their national action plans. By means of these national action plans and through international efforts, particular priority should be placed on reducing infant and maternal mortality rates, reducing malnutrition and illiteracy rates and providing access to safe drinking water and basic education. Whenever so called for, national plans of action should be devised to combat devastating emergencies resulting from natural disasters and armed conflicts and the equally grave problem of children in extreme poverty. Further para 48 urges all states, with the support of international cooperation, to address the acute problem of children under especially difficult circumstances. Exploitation and abuse of children should be actively combated, including by addressing their root causes. Effective measures are required against female infanticide, harmful child labour, sale of children and organs, child prostitution, child pornography, as well as other forms of sexual abuse. This gave an influence to adoptions of optional protocol on the involvement of children in armed conflict and optional protocol on the sale of children, child prostitution and child pornography.

Enforcement Organizations and Mechanisms

A variety of enforcement organizations and mechanisms exist to ensure children's rights. They include the Child Rights Caucus for the United Nations General Assembly Special Session on Children. It was set up to promote full implementation and compliance with the Convention on the Rights of the Child, and to ensure that child rights were given priority during the UN General Assembly Special Session on Children and its Preparatory process. The United Nations Human Rights Council was created "with the hope that it could be more objective, credible and efficient in denouncing human rights violations worldwide than the highly politicized Commission on Human Rights." The NGO Group for the Convention on the Rights of the Child is a coalition of international non-governmental organisations originally formed in 1983 to facilitate the implementation of the United Nations Convention on the Rights of the Child. Many countries around the world have children's rights ombuds people or children's commissioners whose official, governmental duty is to represent the interests of the public by investigating and addressing complaints reported by individual citizens regarding children's rights. Children's ombuds people can also work for a corporation, a newspaper, an NGO, or even for the general public.

The National Commission for Protection of Child Rights (NCPCR), India

The National Commission for Protection of Child Rights (NCPCR) was set up in March 2007 under the Commission for Protection of Child Rights Act, 2005, an Act of Parliament (December 2005) of India. It was set up to protect, promote and defend child rights in the country. The Commission's Mandate is to ensure that all Laws, Policies, Programmes, and Administrative Mechanisms are in consonance with the Child Rights perspective as enshrined in the Constitution of India and also the UN Convention on the Rights of the Child. The Child is defined as a person in the 0 to 18 years age group. The Commission visualises a rights-based perspective flowing into National Policies and Programmes, along with nuanced responses at the State, District and Block levels, taking care of specificities and strengths of each region. In order to touch every child, it seeks a deeper penetration to communities and households and expects that the ground experiences inform the support the field receives from all the authorities at the higher level. Thus the Commission sees an indispensable role for the State, sound institution-building processes, respect for decentralization at the level of the local bodies at the community level and larger societal concern for children and their well-being.

NCPCR emphasises the principle of universality and inviolability of child rights and recognises the tone of urgency in all the child related policies of the country. For the Commission, protection of all children in the 0 to 18 years age group is of equal importance. Thus, policies define priority actions for the most vulnerable children. This includes focus on regions that are backward or on communities or children under certain circumstances, and so on. The NCPCR believes that while in addressing only some children, there could be a fallacy of exclusion of many vulnerable children who may not fall under the defined or targeted categories. In its translation into practice, the task of reaching out to all children gets compromised and a societal tolerance of violation of child rights continues. This would in fact have an impact on the program for the targeted population as well. Therefore, it considers that it is only in building a larger atmosphere in favour of protection of children's rights, that children who are targeted become visible and gain confidence to access their entitlements. Likewise, for the Commission, every right the child enjoys is seen as mutually-reinforcing and interdependent. Therefore the issue of gradation of rights does not arise. A child enjoying all her rights at her 18th year is dependent on the access to all her entitlements from the time she is born. Thus policies interventions assume significance at all stages. For the Commission, all the rights of children are of equal importance.

Constitutional Provisions on Child Rights in India

- **Article 21 A** of Constitution of India: "The State shall provide free and compulsory education to all children of the age of 6-14 years in such manner as the State may by law determine"
- **Article 23 (1)** of Constitution of India: "Traffic in human beings, beggary and other similar forms of forced labour are prohibited and any contravention of this provision shall be an offence punishable in accordance with law"

The National Policy for Children, 2013

India is home to the largest child population in the world. The Constitution of India guarantees Fundamental Rights to all children in the country and empowers the State to make special provisions for children. The Directive Principles of State Policy specifically guide the State in securing the tender age of children from abuse and ensuring that children are given opportunities and facilities to develop in a healthy manner in conditions of freedom and dignity. The State is responsible for ensuring that childhood is protected from exploitation and moral and material abandonment. Declaring its children as the nation's "supremely important asset" in the National Policy for Children, 1974, the Government of India reiterated its commitment to secure the rights of its children by ratifying related international conventions and treaties. These include the Declaration of the Rights of the Child, Universal Declaration of Human Rights and its Covenants, the Convention on the Rights of the Child and its two Optional Protocols, the United Nations Convention on the Rights of Persons with Disabilities, the United Nations Convention against Transnational Organized Crime, the Protocol to Prevent, Suppress and Punish Trafficking in Women and Children, the Hague Convention on Protection of Children and Cooperation in respect of Inter-Country Adoption, and the Convention on the Elimination of All Forms of Discrimination against Women.

The National Policy for Children, 1974 recognised that programmes for children should find prominent place in national plans for the development of human resources, so that children grow up to become robust citizens, physically fit, mentally alert and morally healthy, endowed with the skills and motivations provided by society. The Policy also laid emphasis on equal opportunities for the development of all children during the period of growth. The National Charter for Children, 2003 adopted on 9th February

2004, underlined the intent to secure for every child its inherent right to be a child and enjoy a healthy and happy childhood, to address the root causes that negate the healthy growth and development of children, and to awaken the conscience of the community in the wider societal context to protect children from all forms of abuse, while strengthening the family, society and the Nation.

This Policy is to guide and inform all laws, policies, plans and programmes affecting children. All actions and initiatives of the national, state and local government in all sectors must respect and uphold the principles and provisions of this Policy. Survival, health, nutrition, development, education, protection and participation are the undeniable rights of every child and are the key priorities of this Policy.

The implementation of this Policy will be supported by a comprehensive and reliable knowledge base on all aspects of the status and condition of children. Establishing such a knowledge base would be enabled through child focused research and documentation, both quantitative as well as qualitative. A continuous process of indicator-based child impact assessment and evaluation will be developed, and assessment and evaluation will be carried out on the situation of children in the country, which will inform policies and programmes for children. Professional and technical competence and capability in all aspects of programming, managing, working and caring for children at all levels in all sectors will be ensured through appropriate selection and well planned capacity development initiatives. All duty bearers working with children will be sensitised and oriented on child rights and held accountable for their acts of omission and commission.

The State commits to allocate the required financial, material and human resources, and their efficient and effective use, with transparency and accountability, to implement this Policy. Child budgeting will track allocation and utilisation of resources and their impact on outcomes for children with regard to budgets and expenditures on children by all related Ministries and Departments. A comprehensive review of this Policy will be taken up once in five years in consultation with all stakeholders, including children. The Ministry of Women and Child Development will lead the review process.

The Right of Children to Free and Compulsory Education Act, 2009

The right of children to free and compulsory education act or right to education act (RTE) 2009 which was passed by the Indian parliament on 4 August 2009, describes the modalities of the provision of free and compulsory education for children between 6 and 14 in India under Article 21A of the Indian Constitution. India became one of 135 countries to make education a fundamental right of every child when the act came into force on 1 April 2010. As per this act, Every child between the ages of 6 to 14 years has the right to free and compulsory education. This is stated as per the 86th Constitution Amendment Act of 2002. The right to education act seeks to give effect to this amendment. The government schools shall provide free education to all the children and the schools will be managed by School Management Committees (SMC). Private schools shall admit at least 25% of the children in their schools without any fee. The National Commission for Elementary Education shall be constituted to monitor all aspects of elementary education including quality.

Conclusion

Children have good ideas. They can think of things that adults would not. Furthermore, full respect of the best interests of the child, which is among the key principles in child rights protection, requires that children are given opportunities to voice their opinions on matters that affect them. Children want to be active participants in the decisions being made about them and to feel that their opinions are respected. Fully developed children's rights education means that all members of the school community receive education on the rights of the child. The Convention serves as a values framework for the life and functioning of the school or educational institution and for efforts to promote a more positive school climate and school culture for learning. A core belief in children's rights education is that when children learn about their own basic human rights, this learning serves as an important foundation for their understanding and support of human rights more broadly.

REFERENCES

1. Agarwal (1983). *Implementation of Human Rights Covenants with Special Reference to India*. Allahabad: Kitab Mahal.
2. Batra, T.S. (1979). *Human Rights- A Critique*. New Delhi: Metropolitan Book Co., (P) Ltd.
3. Baxi, U. (Ed.) (1987). *The Right to be Human*. New Delhi: Lancer International.
4. Chand, A. (1985). *Politics of Human Rights and Civil Liberties*. Delhi: UDH Publishers.
5. Government of India (1966). *Education and National Development*. Report of the Education Commission 1964-66. New Delhi: Ministry of Education.
6. Graves, N. (1990). *Teaching for International Understanding, Peace and Human Rights*. Paris: UNESCO.
7. http://en.wikipedia.org/wiki/Children%E2%80%99s_rights_education
8. Ministry of Women and Child development (2012). *The National Policy for Children, 2013*. Gazette of India retrieved from http://wcd.nic.in
9. Naseema, (2012). *Human Rights Education*. New Delhi: Kanishka Publishers.
10. UNESCO (2000).*The Dakar Framework for Action for All: Meeting our Collective Commitments*. Paris: UNESCO.
11. Vandenberg (1990). Ed*ucation as Human Rights: A Theory of Curriculum and Pedagogy*. New Delhi: Teacher's College Press.
12. www.indg.in/primary-education/policiesandschemes/right-to-education-bill

4 Guiding Principles of Adolescence Education

Introduction

This unit is focused on developing an appropriate understanding of the conceptual framework of Adolescence Education. Adolescence Education is an educational response to the needs, concerns and realities of adolescents. This unit describes the realities of Indian adolescents, and adolescence education as a systematic response to address their concerns. Adolescents are a positive resource. They have energy and idealism. Adolescence is a transition period between childhood and adulthood. Adolescents need information and somebody who will answer their questions. Adolescence education is a response to the adolescents' need for authentic information, provided in a safe and friendly atmosphere. India is proud to be home to 327 million young people in the age group of 10-24 (WHO, 2007), and is also responsible for developing this vast human resource in the best possible ways.

Adolescence Education aims to respond to the concerns of adolescents, specifically the ones that are yet to be assimilated by school curriculum in full measure. The overall objective of Adolescence Education is to provide adolescents with accurate, age appropriate and culturally relevant information, promote healthy attitudes and develop skills to enable them to respond to real-life situations effectively. The Main content areas of adolescence education include:

- the process of growing up;
- prevention of HIV and AIDS; and
- prevention of substance/drug Abuse.

Understanding of life skills development as a core objective and as a generic concept, not only related to the selective concerns of adolescents like peer pressure or risk taking behaviour. The need for participatory teaching/transaction methods that build on the experiences of learners rather than didactic and rote teaching-learning methods. One of the major objectives of adolescence education is to develop life skills to empower young people to respond to the real life situations in positive and responsible ways. Life Skills are psycho-social abilities that enable individuals to translate knowledge, attitude and values regarding their concerns into well-informed and healthy behaviours. Empowered with skills; young people are able to take decisions based on a logical process of "what to do, why to do, how to do and when to do."

Needs, Concerns and Realities of Adolescents in India

World Health Organization (WHO) defines that individuals in the age group of 10-19 are known as adolescents, in the age group of 10-24 as young people and in the age group of 15-24 as youth. India has 327 million young people in the age group of 10-24 (WHO, 2007) Eighty three percent young men and 78% young women in the age group 15-24 expressed that they perceived family life education to be important (IIPS: Pop Council Youth survey, 2006-07). Young people (45% boys and 27% girls) voted for teacher as the most appropriate person to transact education on family life matters (IIPS: Pop Council Youth survey, 2006-07). Findings from the National Family Health Survey 3 (NFHS 3, 2005-06) also show that young people are poorly informed on issues related to HIV prevention. Only 28% of young women and 54% of young men in the age group of 15-24 had comprehensive knowledge about HIV/AIDS. This is worrisome in the light of the fact that over 35% of all reported AIDS cases in India occur among young people in the age group of 15-24 years and more than 50% of the new HIV infections occur also among young people (NACO, 2005). Substance abuse among young people is also a matter of concern. Findings from NFHS-3 show that in the age group of 15-24, 40% young men and 5% young women had ever used tobacco, while 20% of young men and 1% of young women had ever consumed alcohol. Although young people are considered healthy, findings from NFHS 3 indicate that a substantial proportion of young people suffer from anaemia (56% of females and 25% of males in the 15-24 age group) that can adversely affect their physical growth, cognitive development, performance in school and at work as well as reproduction.

Guiding Principles of Adolescence Education

Adolescence is conceptualized as a positive stage of life, full of possibilities and potential. It should not be labelled as problematic and traumatic, and adolescents (and the 'peer group') should not be stereotyped in negative ways. Adolescence Education should recognize and respond to the reality that adolescents are heterogeneous: with diversity in terms of urban/rural, caste, class, religion, cultural beliefs, and so on. Adolescence Education should enable adolescents to understand and negotiate existing and constantly changing lived realities. Teachers need to unlearn and learn in order to facilitate the effective transaction of this curricular area. This is relevant in respect of content, attitudes and pedagogical modalities. The programme should enable adolescents to articulate their issues and know their rights, counter shame and fear, build up self-esteem and self-confidence, and develop ability to take on responsibility for self, relationships and (to an extent) society around them. Adolescence education should influence the entire school curriculum and ethos, rather than being an isolated, stand-alone component. The Adolescence Education programme should have inbuilt flexibility- in terms of content and process to be able to respond to dynamic needs of young people.

The programme should empower young people through participatory, process oriented, non-judgemental approaches that build on the experiences of learners, and provide them with opportunities to think critically, analyse and infer learning rather than being prescriptive. Adolescence education should be strongly oriented towards the transformational potential of education, based on principles of equity and social justice rather than having a status-quo orientation.

Life Skills Development: Core Objective of Adolescence Education

Life skills are psycho-social abilities that empower individuals to connect with self as well as others and develop healthy life style and positive behaviours. Life skills equip individuals with competence to manage challenging situations and utilize existing opportunities optimally. These skills enhance coping resources and personal and social competencies of individuals.

- Life skills development is a life-long process that helps individuals grow and mature; build confidence in one's decisions taken on the basis of adequate information and thought and discover sources of strength within and outside.
- It is noteworthy that from times immemorial, every culture and society has invested in educating and empowering its younger generation to lead fulfilling and responsible lives. For example, the *Panchatantra* stories from India have important lessons in life skills enhancement that remain relevant for all generations.
- Education, and particularly school education plays a vital role in life skills development among individuals, as it exposes them to varied experiences in their formative years and has abundant potential to provide them with relevant simulated situations to learn and practice.

- Life skills are generic abilities, which can be effectively integrated in educational processes.
- Transaction approaches primarily focused on participatory and experiential modes of learning are effective for life skills development.

The special attributes that mark adolescence include:

- Rapid physical growth and development.
- Physical, social and psychological maturity, not necessarily at the same time.
- Sexual maturity and onset of sexual activity.
- Urge to experiment/try out new things.
- Development of adult mental processes and adult identity.
- Transition from total socio-economic dependence to relative independence.

Profile of Indian Adolescents

The 2001 census tells us that 20 percent of the billion-strong population of the country would qualify as adolescents (age-group 10-19 years), i.e. every fifth person in this country is an adolescent. A significant aspect of adolescence is related to psychological development. It is a critical period for the development of self-identity. The process of acquiring a sense of self is linked to physiological changes, and also learning to negotiate the social and psychological demands of being young adults. Adolescents are affected by socio-economic disparities prevailing in the country. The National Family Health Survey - 3 (NFHS - 3) indicates high percentage of anaemia (56% of females and 25% of males in the 15-24 age group were anaemic), which affects their physical growth, cognitive development, performance in school and at work as well as reproduction.

A national-level study, 'Youth in India: Situation and Needs 2006-07' conducted by the Population Council, New Delhi and International Institute for Population Sciences, Mumbai, indicates that although most youth preferred to marry after age 18; as many as 19% of young women aged 20-24 were married before age 15, and 49% before age 18. Domestic violence is widely prevalent within marriage, with almost a quarter young (married) women reporting that they had been victims of one or other form of physical violence at some point of time within their marriage.

As high as 47% of women and 16% men reported they have never received any information on sexual matters from anybody. A large proportion of young people (78% young women and 83% young men) were in favour of imparting sex education or family life education to youth. The most commonly cited preferred sources for information were parents, teacher, health care providers and other professionals and friends.

Gender roles are very distinctly defined, and adolescent girls continue to face gender based discrimination. This is evident in the declining sex ratio, incidence of domestic violence, under-age pregnancy, unsafe motherhood and increasing incidence of sexual abuse, abduction and trafficking (UNFPA, 2006). The findings from NFHS-3 do not indicate progressive gender role attitudes; 53% women and 56% men in the 15-24 age group felt that wife beating is justified under specific circumstances. Sexual Harassment in public spaces, institutions of education, in and around home and at the workplace is a well established fact. Child abuse, bullying and ragging are also common and more so among boys.

Adolescence Education: A Response to Adolescent Realities

It is universally accepted that the health needs, and particularly the Reproductive and Sexual Health (ARSH) needs of adolescents, continue to be ignored and neglected. As they stand at the threshold of adulthood, they need authentic knowledge that helps them understand the process of growing up with particular reference to their reproductive and sexual health needs. By developing a critical understanding, they have to be well equipped to cope with the problems which they confront. They need guidance and independence simultaneously, education as well as opportunities to explore life for themselves in order to attain the level of maturity required to make responsible and informed decisions.

Objectives, Themes and Scope of Adolescence Education

The concept of 'adolescence education' was preferred to terms like sex education, sexuality education, family life education, reproductive health education, puberty education, life skills education and AIDS education at the National Seminar on Adolescence Education, organised by National Council of Educational Research and Training (NCERT) in 1993. The National Seminar endorsed the use of the concept of adolescence education and recommended the introduction of "suitable components of adolescence education in the curricula at all stages of schooling" (NCERT, 1994). As a follow up to its recommendations, a General Framework of Adolescence Education was finalised through nationwide consultations focusing on the following three requirements:

- Incorporating all the critical concerns of Adolescent Reproductive and Sexual Health (ARSH) in the specific context of Indian socio-cultural ethos;
- Preparing the scheme of contents suitable to provide adequate coverage to ARSH concerns in consonance with the nature and scope of existing school syllabi of different stages; and
- Identifying curriculum transaction strategies focused on promoting experiential learning suited to the specific needs of this new curricular area.

Analysis of school curriculum showed that some concerns were already incorporated in it. It was, therefore, thought logical for the adolescence education framework to focus on those concerns were not incorporated in the school curriculum. Content analysis of the existing curricula indicated that the three closely interrelated areas – process of growing up during adolescence, prevention of HIV/AIDS and prevention of substance (drug) abuse were not adequately covered in the school curriculum. Although the school syllabi and textbooks contain contents on the biological aspects of the reproduction system; education in these content areas cannot be complete by providing biological information only. There is a need to focus on physiological, emotional and socio-cultural dimensions of adolescent reproductive and sexual health (ARSH) in a holistic manner.

Adolescence education was thus conceptualized as an educational intervention, focusing on critical elements that would enable young people to deal effectively with the issues related to:

- Growing up healthy, including issues related to reproductive and sexual health
- Prevention of HIV/AIDS
- Prevention of substance (drug) abuse

After serious consideration, a consensus has been reached in favour of the introduction of adolescence education in schools with a view to providing authentic knowledge to students regarding the process of growing up, HIV/AIDS and substance (drug) abuse, influencing their attitudes, and developing in them the needed life skills to respond to real-life situations effectively. The 1993-96 version of the framework was missing out the element of life skills. In operationalizing the framework, it was realised that adolescence education should lay emphasis on life skills development, so as to empower adolescents to meet the challenges and optimize opportunities that may come their way. The present revised framework not only lays specific emphasis on life skills development but also conceptualises it based on pedagogical principles.

Arguments For and Against Adolescent Education

Arguments Against: Earlier there were many who did not think it proper to introduce elements relating to sexual development in the school curriculum. Even now such a mindset influences the thinking of some adults. They quite often put forth the following arguments:

- Sex and sexuality are intimately private matters which are not to be discussed in public, and that too with young children. In India individuals have been receiving information about these matters indirectly through different sources available in their respective socio-cultural settings. Therefore, there is no need to introduce such an educational programme in Indian schools.

- If schools start providing knowledge about sexual development, young children will be encouraged to experiment with the newly acquired knowledge. This will promote promiscuity and sexual permissiveness, spoiling the youth and also the school and social environment.
- The regular discussion of sex and sexuality, which is a treasured sublime instinct of human beings, will reduce it to a mundane routine affair. The young students will be desensitised and will not be able to appreciate its sublime value in their future lives.

Arguments For: All these arguments were considered during the process of consensus building for introducing adolescence education in schools:

- It is a myth to regard the socio-cultural traditions of India as a safeguard against irresponsible sexual behaviour of individuals. There is definitely a need to make interventions to enable individuals, including young people to practice responsible behaviour and protect themselves from risky situations.
- A number of studies show that adolescents would like to get accurate information about the changes in their bodies including sexual development. However, discussion on issues related to sexuality is a taboo and there are no reliable sources of information to educate adolescents on these issues. This situation creates anxiety and confusion and generates myths and misconceptions among adolescents about various dimensions of their growing up.
- Since the average age at marriage is increasing, young people have a longer interval between their sexual maturity and marriage. In such a context, it is necessary for school curriculum to equip adolescents with authentic information on sexuality, HIV-AIDS and Sexually Transmitted Infections (STIs). This will enable adolescents to manage their sexual development responsibly and develop a healthy attitude towards sex and sexuality.
- Sexual abuse and exploitation of young girls and boys, and even minors, is a problem in Indian society. These situations demand urgent educational intervention, so that young people are made aware of the need to respect the inviolability of every person, and to safeguard themselves against abuse and exploitation.
- The impact of certain traditional values that used to influence sex-related behaviour of individuals has been diminishing. There is a need to reinforce those social and cultural values that may provide sustenance to responsible sexual behaviour.

Children and adolescents are exposed to sex-related ideas and thoughts, and that too at times in a crude manner, through sources like cinema, film magazines and other periodicals, video parlours, commercial advertisements and certain television programmes. It is necessary to empower adolescents through education, so that they may appreciate and analyse such exposures in a proper perspective.

- The AIDS pandemic has added urgency to introduce adolescence education in schools. Preventive education is necessary to promote behaviour changes which can prevent the spread of HIV infection.
- Studies indicate an increasing incidence of smoking and use of tobacco, alcohol and other harmful substances by young persons. Frequently adolescents tend to see the use of these drugs as part of being grown up. It is, therefore, urgently needed to educate them on the effects of substance (drug) abuse.
- Studies indicate that education about reproductive and sexual health does not encourage students to experiment with their newly acquired knowledge. Rather, it encourages them to have positive attitude towards sex and inculcates in them responsible behaviour.
- The apprehension of teachers that teaching the elements of adolescence education will tarnish their "image" and promote indiscipline among students has been negated by experiences. Wherever teachers are responsive to the needs of adolescent students and help them cope with their problems, the teacher-pupil relation has become better and the school environment has improved.
- Although students always felt the need to get education in sex related matters, parents and teachers had serious apprehensions till very recently. But now a number of needs assessment studies conducted in different States have found that parents and teachers overwhelmingly favour the introduction of adolescence education in schools. The need to emphasise the development of life skills is being recognised on a greater scale.

Conclusion

Adolescence education is a new curricular area which is still undergoing the process of validation. It is yet to be considered as an established uniformly accepted curricular area like the existing subjects taught in schools. Many a time it is equated with sex education and made controversial. The life skills development being its core makes it a still more uncommon area. It, therefore, requires special efforts to adopt the transaction strategies for life skills development into the existing education system. The strategies for the institutionalisation of adolescence education in the education system and methods of curriculum transaction, need to be carefully identified primarily. Orienting school curriculum towards responding to the need for life skill development has basic problem that derives from the difficulties of trying to introduce a curricular area into the existing system which is not so conducive to the popularly employed approaches. It will require a different pedagogy that frames the development of life skills as an educational process.

REFERENCES

1. Fischer, C.M. *et.al*. The Role of Community-Based Organizations in Adolescent Sexual Health Promotion. retrieved from http://hpp.sagepub.com
2. http://en.wikipedia.org/wiki/Adolescence
3. http://mhrd.gov.in/adolesence_education
4. http://sevencounties.org/poc/view_doc.php?type=doc&id=41149&cn=1310
5. http://www.naco.gov.in/upload/NACOinActiion/Advocacy%20Kit.pdf
6. http://www.ncert.nic.in/programmes/aep/pdfs/MODULE%201%20ADOLESCENCE%20EDUCATION%20IN%20INDIA.pdf
7. http://www.unicef.org/india/media_2644.htm
8. http://www.unicef.org/india/media_966.htm
9. MHRD (2004) *Life Skills Modules, Adolescence Education Programme*, MHRD, NACO & UNICEF, Delhi.
10. NCERT & NACO (1994) *AIDS Education In School: A Training Package*, Delhi.
11. NCERT,(2005); *Adolescence Education in Schools- Life skills Development General Framework*; National Population Education Project, Deptt. of Education in Social Science and Humanities, New Delhi, India.
12. Stolz, H.E. *et.al*. Adolescent Religiosity and Psychosocial Functioning: Investigating the Roles of Religious Tradition, National-Ethnic Group, and Gender in *Child Development Research*., Vol. 2013., retrieved from http://www.hindawi.com/journals/cdr
13. Thamarasseri, Ismail. (2008) *Psychological Foundations of Education*. New Delhi: Kanishka Publishers.
14. Thamarasseri, Ismail. (2015). *Adolescence Education*. New Delhi: Dominant Publishers & Distributors (P) Ltd.

5

Life Skills in Adolescence Education

Introduction

Today's adolescents are tomorrows adults and these youth are the human capital of our nation. Life skills is 21st century skills; essential for ensure a better productive society. India is proud to be home to 327 million young people in the age group of 10-24 (WHC, 2007), and is also responsible for developing this vast human resource in the best possible ways. The framework of Adolescence Education incorporates life skills as one of the competencies, perhaps the most critical competency developed and inculcated through education. It is generally believed that a person who is educated is equipped with all the needed abilities including life skills. But in reality this does not happen. Knowing what needs to be done or knowing what needs to be changed does not mean that the learners automatically know how to bring about behaviour changes. It is the Life skills that, if properly developed, provide the know-how and the tools to actualize behaviour change. This unit is focused on developing an appropriate understanding of the conceptual framework of Life Skills in Adolescence Education.

Life Skills requires to be perceived as done in Dakar Framework for Action (World Education Forum, Dakar, Senegal, 2000), that stresses the need for not only psychomotor or practical skills, but also those psychosocial abilities – life skills – that will enable individuals to learn and use knowledge into action, to develop reasoning and analytical strengths, to manage emotions and to live with and relate to others. Life skills are abilities to be developed in every individual to equip them to meet the challenges of life and optimise opportunities to live a healthier, happier, productive and fulfilling life. These include all aspects of wholesome living necessary for adolescents to be equipped in approaching eventual responsibilities in adulthood. Adolescence is a critical period in self-understanding, finding one's way and fitting into the society. Development of self-confidence with a positive self-image is the foundation of responsible adulthood. Providing enabling environments to support adolescents in this critical formative stage is the main mandate in the development of life skills.

Life skills are generic abilities like any other, i.e., knowledge ability, attitude, interest, sentiments, value orientation, and so on. Ongoing education processes have focused solely on academics, and have not adopted an approach that can ensure development of life skills. Life skills can be effectively integrated in educational processes, and the ability for their application in specific contexts can also be developed.

Life Skills are different from other Skills

- Other skills like mechanical skills, livelihood skills, vocational skills or language skills are technical, life skills are psycho-social (personal, social, interpersonal, cognitive, affective and universal) directed towards personal actions or actions towards others;
- Life skills are interpersonal skills empowering individuals to interact with the self as well as others and develop healthy lifestyle and responsive and responsible behaviour; and
- Other skills are product of continued practice, while life skills are developed through interactive experiential learning.

Life Skills Development: Approach Framework

It is important to note that life skills development does not mean development of skills afresh by a set of educational interventions at a particular point of time. Life skills development is an integral part of the all-encompassing process of socialisation that continues throughout human life. School education is an integral part of this process. In fact, individuals apply the acquired life skills in different contexts differently. An individual may have acquired a life skill and she/he may also be equipped with the ability to apply that skill in a context that is fundamentally different from adolescent reproductive and sexual health. For example, an adolescent may be applying thinking skill or communication skill very effectively while interacting with her/his teacher or even peer group during a discussion on say, globalization or environmental pollution, but she/he may not have the ability to apply those skills on an issue related to sex and sexuality or negative peer pressure. Life skills development, therefore, may be more aptly defined as a process of acquiring the ability to apply concerned skills in the specific context and not the development of that skill afresh.

Since life skills are generic by nature, an educational intervention aimed at the development of ability to apply them may be effective only when it is focused on the specific context. The intervention may have to be designed and operationalized differently for different contexts, more particularly for a culturally sensitive context like adolescent reproductive and sexual health concerns. It needs interventions to focus on acquisition of authentic knowledge, development of positive attitude, and empowerment for avoidance of risky behaviour.

The design of educational intervention has to take note of the content area and also specific life skills. Since most of the contents of adolescence education are very sensitive, interventions need to be well conceived for doing justice to the content. Contextually relevant and age appropriate contents should be focused on. It is important to exactly identify which life skills are to be focused and also the reasons for doing so.

In order to organize educational interventions for life skills development effectively, it is important to identify curricular as well as co-curricular activities that have the potential for developing skill application ability. Certain specific activity will be more appropriate than others in respect of a particular life skill. For example, role play can be very appropriate in respect of negotiation skills or interpersonal skills or skills related to empathy.

One activity can be organized to attain different objectives. It is the process of organizing that activity that makes a fundamental difference by providing exact direction for attaining the desired objective. Group discussion may be able to attain knowledge, understanding and even attitude related objectives, but if it is to attain skill development related objectives, it has to be planned and conducted according to a particular process that sustains its focus throughout on skill development. Since life skills development primarily depends through the mode of experiential learning mode, the process of involving learners in the activity is very important.

Integration of Life Skills in Content and Process of Adolescence Education

In order to ensure that the ongoing education system plays a proactive role in life skills development among learners, there is a need to integrate an approach to provide opportunities of experiential learning to them. This approach needs to be integrated right from the stage of curriculum development to syllabi and materials development, transaction of materials, organization of learning experiences and evaluation. All these aspects of education must actualize a process wherein the learner is no longer treated as a passive recipient of information and facts, but is made an active participant in gathering information, understanding issues and problems, examining the alternatives, seeking reasons, making decisions and solving problems.

The study materials, textual and other teaching-learning tools, need to be prepared in experiential learning mode. The materials must not make the learner accept the given knowledge/information/facts, but take her/him through a process wherein the learner constructs her/his knowledge through analysis, reasoning, and deducing conclusions. This change has to be reflected in a big way in the process of teacher preparation, teaching-learning methods and examination reforms.

Adolescence Education Programme in India: National Framework

Adolescence Education Programme (AEP) was launched by the Ministry of Human Resource Development (MHRD in collaboration with National AIDS Control Organisation (NACO), Government of India in 2005 as a follow up of the decisions taken in an Inter-Ministerial Meeting held in October 2004. The Meeting was held in the Office of Hon'ble Minister of Human Resource Development and also attended by Hon'ble Ministers of Health & Family Welfare, Labour, Rural Development, Social Justice and Empowerment and Information & Broadcasting.

However, the AEP was not launched as a completely new educational programme, rather as an initiative to upscale the following three educational programmes that were already being implemented:

- National Population Education Project (NPEP) that was being implemented by 30 States and Union Territories from 1980, having adolescence education as the most important thrust area since 1993-94;
- School AIDS Education Programme (SAEP) being implemented by NACO since 1993-94 through State AIDS Control Societies; and
- The Project on Adolescent Reproductive and Sexual Health (ARSH) in Schools being implemented by 5 national agencies with the support of United Nations Population Fund (UNFPA). But these programmes had limited outreach, covering relatively smaller number of target groups. Adolescence Education Programme was, therefore, launched as an umbrella programme to cover all the secondary and senior secondary schools of the country.

In pursuance of the decisions of the Inter-Ministerial Meeting, the Programme was developed in a series of meetings involving key stakeholders, senior officials from MHRD, NACO, UNICEF and UNFPA. MHRD was identified as the lead agency for the implementation of AEP, with the financial and technical support from NACO, UNICEF and UNFPA. Regional Workshops were organized to have wider consultations with all the States and Union Territories. The process was culminated by the National Meeting of Secretaries of Education & Project Directors SACS on

Adolescence Education, that was jointly organized by MHRD and NACO on 15 June 2005. The Meeting was addressed by Secretary, DS&HE, Secretary, DEE&L, Special Secretary and Director General, NACO, Director, NCERT, Chairman, CBSE, Vice Chancellor, IGNOU, Chairperson, NCTE, Chairperson, NIOS and Country Representative, UNICEF, among several others.

Adolescence Education: Its Evolution

The consensus to introduce adolescence education in schools evolved much earlier (during early 1990s) than the launching of AEP by MHRD/NACO in 2005. National Council of Educational Research and Training had organized a National Seminar on Adolescence Education from 12-13 April, 1993. The term adolescence education was first used as the title of a publication on sex education brought out by UNESCO Principal Regional Office for Asia and the Pacific, Bangkok in 1990. However, NCERT did not simply adopt the nomenclature but developed its specific connotation and delineated the broad framework of the concept in the Seminar. The National Seminar recommended the introduction of "adolescence education into the curricula at all stages of schooling." It was attended by representatives of almost all the stakeholders in the school education system; viz., eminent educationists, psychologists, medical scientists, sexologists, curriculum developers, teacher educators, school principals and teachers, representatives of government and non- governmental organizations involved in sex education, family life education, AIDS education, health education, preventive education against drug abuse and population education, university education, AIIMS, NACO, SCERTs, State Boards, Family Planning Association of India, Parivar Sewa Sanatha, Centre for Social Research, Reproductive Health Foundation and National Institute of Mental Health and Neurosciences, Ministry of Health and Family Welfare, UNESO and UNFPA.

Based on the recommendations of the National Seminar, NCERT developed the General Framework of Adolescence Education, having three major components (Process of growing up during adolescence, HIV/AIDS and drug abuse) with a detailed Scheme of Content. It was done again through nation-wide consultations by organizing Regional Seminars in different parts of the country. These Seminars were attended by various stakeholders in school education in respective regions. Besides having discussions on different aspects of the General Framework, one day was exclusively devoted to taking the views of parents, teachers and adolescent students in every Regional Seminar.

Need of Educational Intervention

It is in this context that the need for an educational intervention has been strongly felt. This need is particularly felt in India, because the school curriculum does not include the crucial elements of reproductive and sexual health such as physical, psychological/mental development especially in the context of sexual development during the period of adolescence, HIV/AIDS and substance (drug) abuse. There are contents on the biological aspects of the reproduction system in the school syllabi and textbooks, but education in these elements cannot be complete by giving simply the biological information. There is a need to focus on physiological, emotional and socio-cultural dimensions of the adolescent reproductive and sexual health (ARSH) in a holistic manner.

Moreover, the greater need is to equip adolescents with life skills, so that they can cope with the challenges and pressures. After serious consideration for rather too long, now a consensus has been reached in favour of the introduction of adolescence education in schools with a view to providing authentic knowledge to students regarding the process of growing up, HIV/AIDS and substance (drug) abuse, influencing their attitude, behaviour and value orientation, and developing in them the needed life skills.

Adolescence Education Programme (AEP)

In view of the above, Adolescence Education Programme (AEP) being implemented by MHRD in collaboration with NACO has specific contextual relevance. The Department of School Education and Literacy, MHRD has positioned AEP as a Centrally Sponsored Scheme. It is being implemented as a key intervention for empowering adolescents to deal with risky situations, preventing new HIV infections, reducing vulnerability to the infection and substance dependence and influencing positive behaviour development. It is designed as an early HIV preventive intervention by providing adolescents with information on Process of Growing up during adolescence, HIV/AIDS and Substance abuse as well as developing in them life skills as the most effective way to stem the spread of the infection as well as substance abuse.

Aims and Objectives of AEP

The Adolescence Education Programme (2005) aims to:

- Reinforce/support development of behaviours that will empower adolescents to make healthy choices.
- Provide opportunities for the reinforcement of existing positive behaviour and strengthening of life skills that enable young people to protect themselves from and to cope with risky situations they encounter in their lives.

The objectives are to ensure that:

- all schools provide accurate age appropriate life skills based adolescence education in a sustained manner to young people (10-18 yrs) in schools;

- every child is equipped with accurate information, knowledge and life skills to protect themselves from HIV and manage adolescent reproductive sexual health (ARSH) issues and concerns;
- all out-of-school adolescents are provided basic information and services on adolescent reproductive and sexual health, HIV prevention and prevention of substance abuse;
- effective integration of adolescence education components in school curriculum as well as the teacher education courses takes place; and
- linkages to youth friendly services are established and resources for additional information are easily accessible.

Outputs

The following five outputs have been specified for AE:

- Organisation of life skills based co-curricular activities in classes IX-XI;
- Integration of adolescence education in syllabi, textbooks and teaching learning processes of school education;
- Integration of adolescence education in the pre-service and in-service teacher education;
- Integration of adolescence education in programmes for out-of-school adolescents and young person's; and
- Incorporation of measures to prevent stigma and discrimination into education policy.

Scheme of Content: Adolescence Education Programme focuses on major contents related to the following three components:

Process of Growing up: This component covers contents on the process of growth and development during adolescence, such as physical growth and development including development of secondary sexual characteristics, psychological developments underscoring self identity, self concept, self esteem, sex drive and attraction towards opposite sex, socio-cultural development including relationships of adolescents with parents, peer group and the opposite sex and gender roles and myths and misconceptions. Critical issues like menstruation and menstrual hygiene, masturbation and the genital hygiene, adolescent pregnancy, nutritional needs of adolescents in general and adolescent girls in particular, major sexually transmitted infections (STIs), reproductive tract infections (RTIs) and adolescent friendly health services (AFHS) are also included in this component.

HIV/AIDS: This component includes contents on causes and consequences of HIV/AIDS, preventive measures, anti-retroviral therapy

(ART), individual and social responsibilities towards HIV/AIDS patients and the services available for prevention of spread of HIV and also for HIV infected persons.

Substance (Drug) Abuse: Under this component are covered the critical mental health concerns and the situations in which adolescents are driven to substance (drug) abuse, commonly abused substances (drugs), consequences of substance abuse, preventive measures, treatment, rehabilitation of drug addicts and individual and social responsibilities.

Target Group: The mandate of the Adolescence Education Programme is to cover all secondary and senior secondary schools, rural, urban and transitional across the country. It covers all students studying at the secondary and senior secondary level in:

- Government, local body and government–aided schools,
- Educational guarantee schemes (alternative innovative schemes, across the country
- All out-of-school children and adolescents being catered to by the adult literacy programmes
- Students of open schooling/open university systems. It covers selected nodal teachers and peer educators of all the secondary and senior secondary schools, concerned educational administrators and other educational functionaries.

The pre-service pupil teachers and teacher educators also constitute its target group. Policy framers, Senior functionaries involved in policy operationalisation, Opinion leaders, Media persons, community leaders and parents are covered through advocacy programmes.

Approach for Transaction: Adolescence education is a new curricular area which is still undergoing the process of validation. It is yet to be considered as an established uniformly accepted curricular area like the existing subjects taught in schools. Many a time it is equated with sex education and made controversial. The life skills development being its core makes it a still more uncommon area. It, therefore, requires special efforts to adopt the transaction strategies for life skills development into the existing education system. The strategies for the institutionalisation of adolescence education in the education system and methods of curriculum transaction, therefore, need to be carefully identified primarily because of the following characteristics of this area:

- Since adolescence education focused primarily on life skills development has emerged as a curricular area in response to the pressing demands emanating from outside the education system, it is considered to be imposed on the education system and hence is often not put through the general curriculum planning and review process. It is often given, if at all it is done, a marginal space within the curriculum.

- It deals with contents that are very sensitive in nature and there is an in-built resistance to these elements. Its content structure is still undergoing the process of validation.
- This educational area focuses on problems confronted by adolescents who have been traditionally treated as a homogeneous group which they are not. The variations in their age-range and their socio-cultural settings indicate their heterogeneous nature. More often than not the elitist and urban bias creeps in the process of its conceptualization, and this creates another set of problems.
- Adolescence education is primarily aimed at influencing the non-cognitive domain and developing life skills among the learners. This needs transactional strategies that create experiential learning situations in consonance with the immediate socio-cultural environment of the learners and are basically interactive.
- Although there is an increasing realisation of the urgency for adolescence education and developing coping skills among adolescents, the age-old inhibitions and perceptible apprehensions in the adult world would require persistent efforts aimed at creating enabling environment for this educational intervention in schools.

Moreover, orienting school curriculum towards responding to the need for life skill development has basic problem that derives from the difficulties of trying to introduce a curricular area into the existing system which is not so conducive to the popularly employed approaches. It will require a different pedagogy that frames the development of life skills as an educational process.

Strategies: In view of the above, the following strategies are adopted under AEP to facilitate the institutionalisation of this curricular area in the content and process of school education and teacher education:

Advocacy: The first and foremost need is to create a favourable environment for acceptance of the urgent need to impart adolescence education in schools. It has been experienced over a period of time that in most cases the resistance to adolescence education has been because of the lack of proper appreciation of the needs of adolescents in the changing context and also of this educational area. This requires advocacy with policy framers, opinion leaders, media persons, curriculum developers, teacher educators, teachers and parents. Suitable strategies such as increasing use of mass media, particularly electronic media and regular interactions with concerned target groups including media persons may be very useful.

Life Skills based Co-Curricular Activities

Adolescence Education Programme provides priority to the organization of life skills based co-curricular activities, even though the integration of adolescence education elements in syllabi and textbooks has the potential to make this educational intervention a permanent part of school curriculum. However, the integration of these elements in syllabi and textbooks at national and state levels may have to wait till they are revised in due course of time. But in view of the urgent need, adolescence education should not be postponed until its elements are integrated in syllabi and textbooks. More importantly, for facilitating and promoting life skills development among adolescents, the transaction of adolescence education in schools are being initiated forthwith by adopting the co-curricular approach. Co-curricular activities focused on life skills development are being organized in schools. Activities contained in Teachers' Work Book may prove very effective in not only providing accurate and adequate information to students but also inculcating in them positive attitude and more importantly developing the needed life skills.

Integration in the School Curriculum

Adolescence education can be effectively transacted only when its elements are integrated in the school curriculum. With a view to facilitating effective integration of adolescence education in the content and process of school education, it is necessary that the framework of adolescence education reflects adolescent reproductive and sexual health concerns relevant to various socio-cultural settings comprehensively. The nature of the existing school curriculum will also be a key determinant. The most important concern to be focused while integrating adolescence education elements in the school curriculum has to be life skills development. The integrated elements have to be specifically oriented towards this concern.

- School syllabi and textbooks of all the subjects have to be reviewed to identify the scope of integration of elements of adolescence education and also the relevant entry points in each subject;
- Needed materials for facilitating effective integration with a focus on life skills development may have to be prepared;
- Intensive orientation of curriculum framers, textbook writers, teacher educators and other concerned educational functionaries will make great contribution;
- The adolescence education contents may then be suitably incorporated in the syllabi and textbooks when they are revised; and

- These elements and the needed transactional methods may be integrated in the teacher education courses.

Major Activity Components: The following major activities are being organized under the Adolescence Education Programme:

Advocacy: Advocacy programmes of varied duration are organized for the crucial target groups at different levels to enable them to appreciate the need for adolescence education and make them aware of different aspects of the programme and motivate them to support the implementation of AEP. The target groups are: policy makers, opinion leaders/legislators, religious/community leaders, educational administrators, media persons, principals/heads of schools, curriculum framers, teachers;

Training: Adolescence education being a new curricular area with certain uniqueness, there is a need to develop capabilities among those who are engaged in its transaction, and more particularly the teachers who are key actors in the successful transaction of this curricular area especially focused on life skills development. The following training activities are, therefore conducted under AEP:

- Training of master trainers who in turn train the teachers, peer educators and other functionaries;
- Intensive training of teachers, peer educators and other functionaries for empowering them to transact this curricular area with ease, competence and need-based culture specific care; and also to hold regular consultations with parents and other critical target groups identified at different levels;
- Organization of life skills focused activities for students in and out of classrooms by teachers/peer educators; and
- Coordination and monitoring of various activities and the Programme.

Implementing Agencies Almost all the institutions engaged in school education, teacher education, adult literacy programmes, innovative education schemes at national, state and district levels are involved in the implementation of this Programme.

National Level: National Core Committee under the Chairmanship of Education Secretary is the highest policy making and monitoring body and National Institute of Open Schooling (NIOS) are implementing AEP supported by UNFPA and conducting activities for effective integration of adolescence education elements in syllabi, textbooks, curricula, study materials, IVRS System and evaluation process. Central Board of Secondary Education (CBSE), *Kendriya Vidyalaya Sangathan* (KVS) and *Navodaya Vidyalaya Sangathan* (NVS) are implementing AEP supported by UNFPA and conducting activities for organizing life skills based co-curricular activities in adolescence education in their respective schools NCERT is coordinating the implementation as well as AEP launched by MHRD including the component of AEP supported by UNFPA and also providing technical backstopping. IGNOU, National Council for Teacher Education (NCTE), Directorate of Adult Education are involved in the implementing of AEP for facilitating integration of adolescence education elements in the content and process of Open University system, pre-service and in-service teacher education and adult education system.

State Level: State Core Committee under the Chairmanship of Education Secretary of State government is the highest policy making and monitoring body at the state level. Adolescence Education Cells in State Council of Educational Research and Training (SCERTs)/State Institute of Education (SIEs)/Directorates of Education are implementing AEP at the state level. State Boards are also involved in this programme. District Education Office/District Institutes of Education and Training (DIETs) are engaged in organization of Activities and monitoring and evaluation of AEP.

Life Skills Development: Core Objective of Adolescence Education

Life skills are psycho-social abilities that empower individuals to connect with self as well as others and develop healthy life style and positive behaviours. Life skills equip individuals with competence to manage challenging situations and utilize existing opportunities optimally. These skills enhance coping resources and personal and social competencies of individuals.

- Life skills development is a life-long process that helps individuals grow and mature; build confidence in one's decisions taken on the basis of adequate information and thought and discover sources of strength within and outside.
- It is noteworthy that from times immemorial, every culture and society has invested in educating and empowering its younger generation to lead fulfilling and responsible lives. For example, the *Panchatantra* stories from India have important lessons in life skills enhancement that remain relevant for all generations.
- Education, and particularly school education plays a vital role in life skills development among individuals, as it exposes them to varied experiences in their formative years and has abundant potential to provide them with relevant simulated situations to learn and practice.
- Life skills are generic abilities, which can be effectively integrated in educational processes.
- Transaction approaches primarily focused on participatory and experiential modes of learning are effective for life skills development.

Conclusion

Adolescence Education is an educational response to the needs, concerns and realities of adolescents. Adolescents are a positive resource. They have energy and idealism. Adolescence is a transition period between childhood and adulthood. Adolescents need information and somebody who will answer their questions. Adolescence education is a response to the adolescents' need for authentic information, provided in a safe and friendly atmosphere. Adolescence education is a new curricular area which is still undergoing the process of validation It is yet to be considered as an established uniformly accepted curricular area like the existing subjects taught in schools. Many a time it is equated with sex education and made controversial. The life skills development being its core makes it a still more uncommon area. It, therefore, requires special efforts to adopt the transaction strategies for life skills development into the existing education system. The strategies for the institutionalisation of adolescence education in the education system and methods of curriculum transaction, need to be carefully identified primarily. Orienting school curriculum towards responding to the need for life skill development has basic problem that derives from the difficulties of trying to introduce a curricular area into the existing system which is not so conducive to the popularly employed approaches. It will require a different pedagogy that frames the development of life skills as an educational process. Life Skills in this context need to be defined as psycho-social abilities that enable individuals to translate knowledge, attitude and values regarding all the concerned issues into action. These related to health, mental health, sexual development, HIV and AIDS and Drug abuse. Life skills development empowers learners to observe the process involving "what to do, why to do, how to do and when to do". It encompasses the ability to build sound, harmonious relationships with self, others and the environment, the ability to act responsibly and safely, the ability to survive under a variety of conditions, and the ability to solve problems.

REFERENCES

1. Fischer, C.M. *et.al. The Role of Community-Based Organizations in Adolescent Sexual Health Promotion.* retrieved from http://hpp.sagepub.com
2. http://en.wikipedia.org/wiki/Adolescence
3. http://mhrd.gov.in/adolesence_education
4. http://sevencounties.org/poc/view_doc.php?type=doc&id=41149&cn=1310
5. http://www.naco.gov.in/upload/NACOinActiion/Advocacy%20Kit.pdf
6. http://www.ncert.nic.in/programmes/aep/pdfs/MODULE%201%20ADOLESCENCE%20EDUCATION%20IN%20INDIA.pdf
7. http://www.unicef.org/india/media_2644.htm

8. http://www.unicef.org/india/media_966.htm
9. MHRD (2004) *Life Skills Modules, Adolescence Education Programme*, MHRD, NACO & UNICEF, Delhi.
10. NCERT & NACO (1994) *AIDS Education In School: A Training Package*, Delhi
11. NCERT. (2005) *Adolescence Education in Schools- Life skills Development General Framework; National Population Education Project*, Departmnet of Education in Social Science and Humanities, New Delhi, India.
12. Stolz, H.E. *et.al*. Adolescent Religiosity and Psychosocial Functioning: Investigating the Roles of Religious Tradition, National-Ethnic Group, and Gender in *Child Development Research*., Vol.2013., retrieved from http://www.hindawi.com/journals/cdr
13. Thamarasseri, Ismail. (2008) *Psychological Foundations of Education*. New Delhi: Kanishka Publishers.
14. Thamarasseri, Ismail. (2015). *Adolescence Education*. New Delhi: Dominant Publishers & Distributors (P) Ltd.
15. Thomas, D.L and Carver, C. "Religion and Adolescent Social Competence," in *Latter-day Saint Social Life: Social Research on the LDS Church and its Members* (Provo, UT: Religious Studies Center, Brigham Young University, 1998), 373–400. retrieved from http://rsc.byu.edu/archived

6

Educating for Character

Introduction

It is widely agreed that the primary function of education is concerned with values. Education transmits cultural and social values to the students. Along with that education helps children to cultivate values. The schools collaborate and support the values that have been transmitted from the home through practical demonstration by good virtues by the teacher. The family is vested with the responsibility of educating the offspring. The parents and teachers are required to work collaboratively to mould the child in school. The parents as well as the teachers in school are to collectively grant the child psychological development by providing him with security and love for emotional stability. Schools convey to children what is expected of them, what is right and wrong. It is often claimed that values are caught rather than taught; through their ethos, schools socialize children into patterns of moral behaviour. We know how education influences culture, society and human behaviour. Social living is intertwined with moral evaluations and values. These values help the members of any given society to live in a peaceful way. It also helps the existing resources to be distributed equitably and fairly. This brings about progress, growth and development in a society and country. This chapter will look in detail on the values associated with education. In this chapter, character and values alongside educational institutions are discussed.

Values are important and lasting beliefs or ideals shared by the members of a culture about what is good or bad and desirable or undesirable. Values have major influence on a person's behaviour and attitude and serve as broad guidelines in all situations. Some common values are fairness, innovation, community involvement, love, sharing, honesty, patriotism, loyalty, truthfulness and so forth. In any country there are vices within the society that are against the moral values. These vices include corruption, armed robbery, stealing, raping, cultism, examination malpractices, rioting, assassination, touting etc. Morality is concerned with all relationships between persons in human society. Moral education need to embrace the societal values and virtues which are rooted in culture. There are variations in cultural origin. What is acceptable in some cultural setting are under questioning in other places. Values like honesty, loyalty, patriotism, faithfulness, obedience, respect, truthfulness, love, unity, cooperation and so on need to be properly taught and stressed in the school. Moral values are moral exhibitions that are acceptable, cherished, appreciated and appraised by the members of any given society. At the same time it is the function of education to teach students to abstain from what is not moral. This need to constitute crucial aspect of body of knowledge and should be taught at the secondary levels in all courses.

Folklores and legend, fable and proverb, parable and allegory, drama and role playing, film and films-strip, newspaper and magazine, television and advertising all may be used as vehicles for moral learning. The aim of all such moral education is not simply to enlarge moral knowledge. It seeks to provide practical experience of situation through which children may learn the basic principles and values involved in living together. It is also concerned with insight, imagination, understanding, emotion and with reasoning. It involves the shaping of attitudes and the development of moral skills. The heart of morality is care and concern for others and hence the basic theme of all moral education is self, others and the relationship between self and others. The societal values like honesty, patriotism, loyalty, truthfulness, love, sharing and so on are to be taught by teachers. This develops moral attitudes in the students in order to have a stable society. Such values are exhibited as acceptable behaviour in the larger society. Indirectly, the teacher serves as a source of moral values through the demonstration of positive virtues for children to learn.

Character and Education: Historically, education systems in every country of the world have had two primary objectives. i.e., To help young people master the skills of literacy and numeracy and to help them become good people. Plato who taught that we educate people to make them good because good people behave nobly. Plato believed that the State would ultimately reflect the character of its citizens. Plato concluded that the renewal of the State is dependent upon the development of the individual character, especially that of the leader. Schools have an extraordinary opportunity to help young people make good decisions for the right reasons by assisting them to make the connection between their character and their conduct.

Rooted in the Greek word 'Charakter', the term character has come to mean the constellation of strengths and weaknesses that form and reveal who we are ... Assessing our character means taking an inventory of our dominant thoughts and actions. The traditional understanding from the Hebrews and Greeks onward is that character is the inner form that makes anyone or anything what it is - whether a person, a wine, or a period in history. Character is distinct from such concepts as personality, image, or reputation. Applied to a person it is the essential stuff that one is made of, the inner reality in which thoughts, speech, decisions and relationships are rooted. As such, character determines behaviour just as behaviour demonstrates character.

Historically, education systems in every country of the world have had two primary objectives, i.e., To help young people master the skills of literacy and numeracy and to help them become good people. Those twin objectives go back through the centuries to Plato who taught that we educate people to make them good because good people behave nobly. Plato believed that the State would ultimately reflect the character of its citizens: States are as people are: they grow out of human character. Plato concluded that the renewal of the State is dependent upon the development of the individual character, especially that of the leader. Schools have an extraordinary opportunity to help young people make good decisions for the right reasons by assisting them to make the connection between their character and their conduct. The best character education inspires young people by making them keenly aware that it is their own character at stake. The reality is that young people feel pressure to make the right decisions but do not know how. Attending to that involves character education.

Character Education: Character education is the deliberate process of developing dispositions and habits that enable us to lead fulfilling lives and build a better world. Character education is at least as old as recorded history. Its advent probably coincides with the beginning of civilization, for it is difficult to sustain a civil society without educating for character. Historically, civilizations passed on their cultural values to succeeding generations as a means of cultural preservation. Until the later decades of the twentieth century character education, or character training, was seen as an essential component of schooling. The historical view which remains valid is that character is taught by precept and example. The cornerstones of character are primarily transmitted through relationships and the culture of a school. The key to effectiveness is not programmes or additions to the curriculum but the creation of a school culture in which the precepts of character are taught, modelled, experienced, advocated and celebrated. Character must inform and influence everything that happens in a school, whether in the principal's office, the sports field, the library or the classroom.

The Demise of Character Education: This total development of human personality includes intellectual and moral development. Most of the present day school and college curriculum only aim at intellectual development. The demise of character education took place during the latter decades of the twentieth century. There are two important questions that need to be asked about the demise of character education. Was character education ever refuted and if so by whom, where and how conclusively? Did character education merely die away as fashions do? If it was the latter, this tells us nothing about its merit or falsehood. The fear of indoctrination loomed large in the demise of character training. Curriculum developers, strongly influenced by psychology and sociology, felt that in a pluralist liberal democracy it was inappropriate to promote one set of values that may violate the beliefs, values and rights of those holding different views. From the 1960's character education gave way to values education. Values are concepts that we hold to be important. Unlike virtues, values can be good or bad, objective or subjective, principle or preference. An ethically good value such as compassion only becomes a virtue, when we develop the motivation and skills to act on it.

Moral values and home: The child receives the greatest and most influential part of his/her learning that will shape his moral development at home. Such direct moral education will be both systematic, casual and episodic. From home and family the child learns the do's and don'ts of social living. The family educates the child on the immediate experiences. Conversely, when there is disagreement between the shared values of the school and home the child's behaviour tend not to be in conformity with the school environment. School demands a new kind of behaviour which does not make sense in the home.

Moral Values and Religion: While most children are exposed to moral values in the home and school, just a few of the children learn the influence of the religious houses on moral values. Religious houses educate children in many matters. Direct, explicit moral instruction in education has been part of our national tradition. Traditionally, moral teaching has been given in the form of abstract principles. The greatest weakness of moral teaching is the conflict of values.

Difference between values and character education: There is an important difference between values education and character education that is not widely understood. Values education is primarily concerned with the quality of students' thinking. Character education is primarily concerned with the quality of students' behaviour. It became the overriding concern of values education that programmes should not favour any particular religious or philosophical point of view. Programmes and approaches have been developed which presented as being neutral and without religious or moralistic bias.

It was seen as important that any values teaching be non-sectarian and non-doctrinaire. The outcome has been that young people, regardless of their social, racial and economic background, have absorbed the unmistakable message that right and wrong are relative, that they must not be judgmental, that what is right for one person may be wrong for another. Right and wrong are personal values, never objective, and always dependent upon time, place and circumstance. This is not a neutral position but the doctrine of situation ethics; moral and cultural relativism.

Curriculum developers in an attempt to eliminate doctrinal bias simply traded perceived indoctrination with the traditional upstanding that there are core universal values for indoctrination in the ideology of ethical relativism. Neutrality in values education is an unachievable aim. Schools must promote some moral values if they are to work at all. Everything a school does teaches values. Whether it is the way the principal treats her staff, the way the class teacher relates to her students, the way the school allows students to treat each other or whether or not the school chooses to discuss moral issues. The best teachers and the best schools have always worked to build character in their students. However, in recent decades, they have been thwarted by theoretical constructions like moral relativism which do not work in practice and deny the wisdom of the ages.

Values and School: Schools have great influence on the moral values and the transmission of such values to children. But compared to home schools have less opportunities to influence the child. It has been a major debate in the educational studies that home and school can cultivate different moral values on a child. This is true especially in the case of societies with caste and class differences. An example of this can be seen in working class or lower class students studying in schools where middle class values are taught. Lower caste children attending school with upper caste students may experience a clash of values. However we cannot neglect the moral impact schools and teachers have on students. Explicit moral education may be both systematic and episodic in the school too. In the school assembly, there is frequent assertion of moral values within the context of actual situations arising from school life. In the classroom there are frequent on-the-spot injunctions to individuals. Also some schools teach students "moral science". This helps the student to understand and absorb moral values in a clear and better way. Teacher is a moral figure for a student. The individual teacher must have immense moral influence on a student like the parent. The teacher is expected to behave as a model to the students. When a student starts identifying with teachers and admiring them, it can be a powerful influence. It is formed by relationship with the school community, the head teacher playing an inevitably leading part. Relationships among the staff between staff and pupils and among pupils themselves are all involved. The school discipline also can influence the moral character of students.

Character education in schools: In recent years, in countries all over the world, there has been a resurgence of character education. Like all genuine reforms character education has started at the grassroots and has not been imposed by education jurisdictions. To date the restoration of character education has been overwhelmingly in primary schools. This is because it is widely recognised that core values are learned at a young age.

Conclusion

In this chapter morality and moral education discussed alongside schooling. The schools collaborate and support the values that have been transmitted from the home through practical demonstration by good virtues by the teacher. The family is vested with the responsibility of educating the offspring. The parents and teachers are required to work collaboratively to mould the child in school. Nearly a hundred years ago Swami Vivekananda showed the close connection between culture and education. Wherever there is a great culture, we will find behind it, a highly developed system of education. Ancient India produces a great culture because it developed a wonderful system of education.

REFERENCES

1. Bull, N.J. (1973) *Moral Education*. Great Britain; Redwood Press.
2. *Connecting Character and Conduct*., Central North Island Secondary School's Deputy and Assistant Principals' Conference Wairakei Resort, Taupo. 21-23 June 2006. John Heenan., retrieved from http://cornerstonevalues.org/conduct.html
3. http://www.businessdictionary.com/definition/values.html#ixzz3KdmtXi34
4. Patteti, A.P., & Thamarasseri, Ismail. (Eds.) (2015). *Education and Human Values*. New Delhi: APH Publishing Corp.
5. Randall R.C. (2003). A *Companion to the Philosophy of Education*. Malden, MA: Blackwell.
6. Thamarasseri, Ismail. (2013). *Value Education*. New Delhi: APH Publishing Corp.
7. The John Templeton Foundation (Eds.). (1999). *Colleges that Encourage Character Development*. Radnor, PA: The John Templeton Foundation. Retrieved on 12-11-2014 from http://www.livingvalues.net/ reference/docs-pdf/Making_the_Case_for_ValuesCharacter_Education.pdf

7

The Worth of Yoga Philosophy

Introduction

All human societies, past and present, have had a vested interest in education; and some wits have claimed that teaching (at its best an educational activity) is the second oldest profession. While not all societies channel sufficient resources into support for educational activities and institutions, all at the very least acknowledge their centrality - and for good reasons. For one thing, it is obvious that children are born illiterate and innumerate, and ignorant of the norms and cultural achievements of the community or society into which they have been thrust; but with the help of professional teachers and the dedicated amateurs in their families and immediate environs (and with the aid, too, of educational resources made available through the media and nowadays the internet), within a few years they can read, write, calculate, and act (at least often) in culturally-appropriate ways. Some learn these skills with more facility than others, and so education also serves as a social-sorting mechanism and undoubtedly has enormous impact on the economic fate of the individual. Put more abstractly, at its best education equips individuals with the skills and substantive knowledge that allows them to define and to pursue their own goals, and also allows them to participate in the life of their community as full-fledged, autonomous citizens. Equips individuals with the skills and substantive knowledge that allows them to define and to pursue their own goals, and also allows them to participate in the life of their community as full-fledged, autonomous citizens.

The philosophy of education plays an important role in providing direction to education on the various issues as well as providing a theory of knowledge for education to work upon. Philosophy of education is essentially a method of approaching educational experience rather than a body of conclusions. It is the specific method which makes it philosophical.

Philosophical method is critical, comprehensive and synthetic. In brief, it is a philosophical process of solving educational problems through philosophical method, from a philosophical attitude to arrive at philosophical conclusions and results. Thus, it aims at achieving general as well as comprehensive results.

The Indian Schools of Philosophy

The Indian schools of philosophy may be classified broadly into two Asthika (orthodox) and Nastika (heterodox). The first group believed in the Vedas and the second school rejected the Vedas. The first one's are called the Asthika systems which have the schools of Mimansa, Vedanta, Sankhya, Yoga, Nyaya and Vaisesika. The latter schools are Charvaka, Buddha and Jaina. Eastern schools of philosophy Eastern philosophies are concerned with all aspects of life. Indian philosophies both orthodox and heterodox are more concerned with the perennial problems of life. So philosophy is - Tattva Darshan or vision of life. Let us outline, now, briefly the salient features of the Indian philosophical tradition.

- Emphasizing ritualistic aspect (mimamsa)
- Indian schools of philosophy
- Nastika (heterodox school) (Charvaka, Buddha, Jaina)
- Asthika (conventional school)
- Based on Vedic text
- Based on independent grounds (Sankhya, Yoga, Nyaya, Vaisesika)
- Emphasizing speculative aspect (Vedanta)

Since time honoured the lore of Yoga was developed and refined by the Indian sages in search of the real-most state of human nature. In course of time that traditionally evolved system of Yoga has been a science of consciousness development and finally in modern time yoga was seen as the science of possibilities, latent within oneself and helpful in dealing with crucial problems of human life. After the popularization of health promotion potentials of Yoga practices among masses, certain other applied aspects of the yoga system, concerned with human resource development, have been remained to be substantiated scientifically. That's why modern educationists are taking interest in improving the quality of education with the help of yoga system. It is seriously being felt that besides the development of national strength and scientific mentality among the students, the aim of education should be the liberation of mind and soul as well.

1. The Indian philosophical schools have developed more a synthetic outlook. There is no separate treatment of ontology (Theory of Reality), Epistemology (Theory of Knowledge), or Ethics and Aesthetics as distinct branches of philosophy. These questions

are approached generally and relatively, some schools stressing more the metaphysical point and some the logical approach to knowledge.

2. Indian philosophical tradition is indifferent to History. Every attempt is made to go into contribution and content of each school by clear exposition and sequential arrangement of things.
3. The underlying spiritual and moral basis is uniform to all the schools generally, except perhaps the philosophy of Charvaka or the materialistic philosophy.
4. Philosophy is a practical necessity for understanding how life can be used. The broad human ends (Purusharthas) are Dharma, Arhta, Kama and Moksha. These are far different from mere intellectual pursuits.
5. Indian philosophy starts with a pessimistic note but builds up a positive approach to realize one's values in life.
6. The doctrine of Karma or a doctrine of action finds a firm faith. The doctrine of births and deaths is common to Vedic Buddhist and Jaina tradition.
7. There is a reference to the universal stage outside the individual self. The content of Para-Brahma is the external universal transcendental edition of the spiritual development of the individual.
8. The terms - Bondage and liberation are used in the sense that the former means the cycle of births and deaths and latter means release from the process.
9. Self-control and concentration are needed to remove passions and develop techniques of yoga and contemplation.
10. The highest aim of life is *Moksha* or *Nirvane* which means liberation positively as the eternal bliss and negatively as destruction of all sufferings.

Concept of Yoga

It is one of the six ancient Indian philosophy other being (Nyaya, Vaisishika, Mimansa, Vedanta and Sankhya). The word Yoga is derived from the word 'YUJ' which means to unite or to combine or to bind yoke with the individual self with the universal self. To bring out the balance & harmony on every level viz. physical, mental & spiritual to transform human into super human. The types of Yoga are:

- Bhaktiyoga
- Gyanayoga
- Karmayoga

- Mantrayoga
- Layayoga

To attain physical, moral, mental and spiritual perfection, the following eight fold steps of yoga discipline are recommended which help in controlling and sublimating attachment which distract the body and mind:

- **Yama:** It is discipline to control will-power. It includes restraint of injury to anyone through thought, word or deed. Absentism from falsehood (satya), from stealing (asteya), from passions and lust, from greed and avarice (aparigraha).
- **Niyama:** It is moral culture and aims at cultivation of good habits. Individual discipline, regulates one's own behaviour. It leads to satisfaction.
- **Asana:** It means steady & comfortable posture. Yogic posture does not involve physical strain or violence, but in turn tones up our body & mind. Reduces our fatigue, soothing nervous system and discipline of the mind.
- **Pranayama:** controlling breath to win overtime, is the discipline of breath control. It aims at regulation of inhalation, retention and exhalation of breath. Not only beneficial to health but also conducive to concentration and meditation.
- **Pratyahara:** controlling senses from their objects. Withdrawal of senses and turning the senses inwards.
- **Dharna:** It is the discipline of fixing the mind without any modification on the object of meditation.
- **Dhyana:** Dhyana means meditation, the steady contemplation of the object of meditation without any break. Concentrating on a point to reach higher self.
- **Samadhi:** It is the state of mind in which contemplative consciousness disappears and has no awareness of itself.

Thus samadhi is ultimate goal of life, being in that state means being in universe. The first five are external aids to yoga while last three are internal aids. The remarkable part of vaidic literature, Kathopanishad elucidates that Yoga is a system of holistic life where all the facets of human life as well of personality get due consideration as inevitable elements of a whole system. In Bhagwad-Gita, composed by the sage Ved-Vyasa, the practical implication of Yoga in active life situations has been wonderfully elaborated. In the modern period, after having been redefined as a system of modern sciences, yoga is presently being defined as a system of personality development, transformation of consciousness and integration within the human system leading to complete well-being. The outstanding figure of contemporary Yoga, Sri Aurobindho defined yoga as a methodical effort towards self- perfection. It is a process by which the limitations and imperfections in man are washed away which result into all round personality development at the physical, mental, intellectual emotional and spiritual levels. There is a great relationship between holistic health and yoga has been proved by present scientists, educationists, psychologist not only in India but by the practitioners all over the world.

Educational Implications of Yoga

Commonly, the term Yoga Education has been referred to as the training and teaching process of Yoga, though it should also be seen as the application of Yoga techniques to bestow better support to the education process. The target of both the disciplines is the same and that is enhancement of socially useful potentials of human personality. To achieve this target, the system of Yoga lays foundation stones whereupon the education system may flourish in all areas. Modern educationists are taking interest in improving the quality of education with the help of yoga system. Yoga in education should lead to the development of harmonious personality and behaviour at all levels. An atmosphere needs to be created where the students study yoga with their own enthusiasm. To the whole the higher level of education is the fittest for integration of yoga. In the current Indian perspective, the role to be played by the education system is facing new challenges. Normally the main aims of education have been the physical, psychological, interpersonal, professional and spiritual refinement of a personality. In modern Indian perspective it is deemed that the system of education should also be helpful in the attainment of the objectives of socialism and democracy mentioned in Indian constitution too. Besides, to attain refinement at the level of thoughts (intellectual development) and feelings (affective aspect), contributing to the development of national character and scientific mentality among the people, at present it is seriously being felt that the aim of education should also include the liberation of mind and soul as well. Acharya Vinobha Bhave, the spiritual heir of Mahatma Gandhi suggested the same that Education in India should be based on three principles i.e. *Yoga* (spiritual training), *Udyoga* (vocational training) and *Sahayoga* (social training)

Areas of Educational Processes

Certain thrust areas positively concerned with educational process have been identified, where the potential of yogic practices are duly proved: Treatment of physical difficulties. Improvement of mental health, and developing resistance to strain. Promotion of emotional balances and control on Hyperactivity.

Positive aspects of yoga

- Promotion of willpower
- Development of perseverance in students
- Education and training about inner self
- Unfolding creative consciousness
- Promotion of uniqueness or talent in the students

Aims of Education

- Comprehensive development of Human personality
- Free child from bodily, mental and supernatural miseries
- Physical, mental, intellectual and spiritual growth
- Moral preparation of pupil
- Understanding of human nature
- Development of scientific attitude and logical and intellectual faculties

Teacher and Taught

- Great importance to teacher
- Not only a theoretician but also a demonstrator
- Give practical demonstration to the student (scientific notion)
- Teacher has power of knowledge, power of will and power of action.
- Role is that of scientist in our age

Student

- Surrender to his teacher for his total cure
- Without teacher nothing can be obtained by the student.

Curriculum

- Not explicitly laid down
- System stands for psycho-physical training of human child
- Provides literature which arouses interest amongst students in moral life.
- Embodies such specific sciences as medicine, clinical psychology, social sciences.
- Yoga approves all those subjects which deal with human physiology, true human nature and hidden laws of nature.
- Comprehensive.
- Most appropriate to the evolution of individual and society.
- If society are highly evolved divine culture can be happily fostered.

Methods of Education

- *cittavrthinirodha* (concentration/meditation) involves right cognition, wrong cognition, imagination, memory.
- Concentration as the most essential method.
- Scientific attitude development method.
- Yoga adopts not only the scientific attitude but also the Programmatic one.
- The system also believes in Discriminative method in acquiring knowledge.
- The law of Association in education constitutes great importance in the Yoga.

Discipline

- Education & Discipline are identical.
- Discipline is the means of which yoga is the aim.
- One has to discipline oneself bodily, mentally and intellectually whether he is a teacher or taught so that he may learn. (Teacher & Taught both)
- Disciplining of body and mind is the core of educational process.

Education system not only in India but the modern globalizing world also really is in great need of taking help of yoga system. Therefore it is high time to think seriously on inclusion of yoga and yogic values in education system.

Self education (education of self-realization): Yoga renders self education. It is nothing but education of self awareness. Yoga teaches us how to live with wisdom, not with the worldly orientations, present education system should inculcate this yogic value intensively. Yoga system can impart progressive training for the development of self awareness and educate us about the realities of our being and becoming.

Pursuit of the transcendental state of Psyche: The paramount aim of yoga system is the pursuit of the transcendental state of psyche i.e. Nidhidhyasana, assumed as an essential aspect of the ancient Indian system of study and education. Samadhi leads to the Nidhidhyasana state which further escorts the wisdom. The experience of Samadhi is not a very difficult or rare stage. Like other components of yoga it is also attainable. Samadhi is a state of consciousness, which begets energy, awareness and delight to the experiencing being for his/her creative thoughts and actions. Moreover, the real creativity is impossible to achieve without attaining Samadhi state. A creative Samadhi is again hard to achieve without adopting high moral values in daily life.

Samadhi (transcendental state) further leads to wisdom: Yoga teaches how to attain wisdom. Knowledge through real vision or wisdom, accomplished by profound meditation, directed to the Samadhi is the real attainment. Learning through mind and senses is a shallow class of knowledge, which leads to complexity. In most of the institutions today, we find that majority of the student are growing with a complexity. Complex living patterns leads to tensions. Methods of peaceful living are not being included in present education system.

Development of General Awareness: The objectives of Yoga, besides causing physical, mental and spiritual enfoldment in an individual, are also the inculcation of social and ecological awareness within oneself. Yoga system emphasizes on awareness of very subtle aspects, hardly attainable subject of single pointed focus. It leads to the awareness of the external environment in its fullest extent and awareness of the external environment in its full depth as well as awareness of internal environment in its full depth as well as awareness of those aspects, which are beyond internal and external attainability. Normally people are so absorbed in self-centred endeavours and materialistic sensual enjoyments around their world that they are unable to see the pros and cons or good and bad effects of their conducts. With the awareness of Yogic values, slowly one experiences the joy present in his surrounding and after a time finds himself deeply connected with his external environment and starts appreciating the truths of ecology.. so the general awareness leading to the deeper appreciation and realizations should be the essence of yoga in education.

Promotion of will Power and Perseverance: The path of Yoga is a test as well as the training of will power. Will power is a quality that plays its major role in every creative performance and success.

Management of Mental Health: In the Eight-limbic system of yoga, Patanjali recommended the observance of Yama and Niyama, for the management of conscious emotional conflicts, whereas, as far as the subconscious emotional are concerned he recommended Asana and Pranayama. Stability of body, brought about by the practice of Asana may lead to the emotional stability and psychological well-being. Many psychologists on the basis of their experimental results and clinical experiences found that Yoga is an effective instrument of modification of human behaviour.

Treatment of Physical Difficulties: From the period of later Upanishads it was duly emphasized that the practice of yogic postures and yogic breathing, in addition to mental and ethical disorders are also able to alleviate physical pains and problems.

Management of Stress Disorders: Stress can be controlled by recommended Yogic techniques. Yoga appears as a system of self-healing, causes remarkable reduction in anxiety and hypertension.

Conclusion

The chief task of philosophy is to determine 'what constitutes a life worth living'. The chief task of education is 'to make life worth living'. Therefore the relationship between philosophy and education is very close. Philosophy tells the goal and essentials of good life. Education tells the means to achieve those goals and learn those essentials of good life. Education is a growing science and its foundations are to be explored for a study of the subject as an inter-disciplinary approach. Philosophy is the corner stone of the foundation of Education. But this does not mean that education should be enslaved to philosophy or some set of values created by human society. Philosophy should be interpreted as a vision in a wider prospective. This being so, education should be wedded to some philosophy in general. We need some frames of reference in which education has to fit. There have been various schools of philosophy presenting their views with much optimism. Education is the process of enabling people not merely does live but to live adequately. There are various facts of education: Academic, Aesthetic, Moral, Physical, Social and Spiritual. Theories of education have been formulated and different values emphasized. Every educational practice is illuminated with the backdrop of philosophy. The speculative, normative and critical function of philosophy affects not only the direction of moral guidance that the teacher gives but also affects the direction of moral guidance that the teacher gives but also affects the direction and the emphasis of the curriculum, the colour of the teachers attitudes from day to day, even from hour to hour.

REFERENCES

1. Aggrawal, J. C. (1996). *Theory and Principles of Education*. New Delhi: Vikas Publishing House.
2. Brunacher, J.S. (1962). *Eclectic Philosophy of Education*, New Jersey: Prentice Hall, Engellwood Cliffs.
3. Coombs, P.H. (1985). *The World Crisis in Education*. New York: Oxford University Press.
4. Dhavan, M.L. (2005). *Philosophy of Education*. Delhi: Isha Books.
5. Ghanta, R. & Dash, B.N. (2006). *Foundations of Education*. Hyderabad: Neelkamal Publications (P) Ltd.
6. Kar, N.K. (1996). *Value Education – A Philosophical Study*. Ambala: The Associated Publication.
7. Kilpatrick, W.H. (1934). *Source Book in the Philosophy of Education*. New York, McMillan and Company.
8. Pandey, R.S. *An Introduction to Major Philosophers of Education*. Agra: Vinod Pustak Mandir.
9. Passi, B.K. (2004). *Value Education*. Agra: National Psychological Corporation.

10. Radhakrishnan, S. & Moore. *Source Book of Indian Philosophy*. Allen and Uncoin.
11. Rena, R. (1971). *Introduction to Indian Philosophy*. New Delhi: Tata Mac Graw Hill.
12. *Scope of Philosophy of Education.*, Retrieved on 27-08-2015 from http://archive.mu.ac.in/myweb_test/ma%20edu/M.A.%20Edu.%20Philosophy.pdf
13. Sharma, R.N. (2000). *Text Book of Educational Philosophy*. New Delhi: Kanishka Publishers.
14. Vivekananda (1982). *Complete Works of Swami Vivekananda* (Vol. V). Advits Publishers.

8 Evaluation of Schools and Quality Assurance of Education

Introduction

The scope of evaluation in schools extends to almost all the areas of pupils' personality Development. It should include both scholastic and non-scholastic areas, i.e. it should be Comprehensive in nature. This is in line with the goals of education. Evaluation is continuous and reveals the strengths and weakness of pupils more frequently, so that the pupils have better opportunity to understand and improve themselves. It also provides feedback to him teachers for modifying their teaching strategies. In this chapter you will study about the internal and external evaluation and commonly used devices for assessment. This chapter also deals with the maintenance of Quality assurance in evaluation and possibilities of blending internal and external evaluation especially at elementary level.

The relationship between the internal and external evaluation of educational institutions has long been a subject of much discussion with regard to thinking on the subject of quality assurance in education. In many countries, External evaluations in the form of school audits, organized by e.g. the Inspectorate, appear always to have enjoyed a somewhat bizarre existence. While everyone accepts the need for them, the way in which these have been carried out has always been heavily criticised (Norton Grubb, 1999; Nevo, 2001). For this reason - and also in response to recent trends with regard to decentralization and increasing autonomy for schools across the globe- evaluation methods have been developed in many countries which permit more participatory and self-directed forms of evaluation (Hara, 2008). The development of mechanism for external and internal evaluation have been systematically encouraged by governments, the media and perhaps most influentially by trans-national agencies such as the OECD and the World Bank (Martin, 2005). Universities, educational support organisations and other entities have developed tools and methodologies to enable schools to evaluate educational quality autonomously. However, although the existence of self-evaluations is welcomed, the quality of these self-evaluations is nonetheless open to question (Vanhoof, 2005). As long as schools are financed by governments, monitoring systems will always have to be devised and schools will have to render account. The precise form which this ought to take is currently subject to considerable change, however (Mahieu, 2005). A trend in many countries is that the primary responsibility for educational quality lies with the school. The withdrawal of government is making schools increasingly autonomous in terms of their freedom to formulate and conduct their own policy. In return for this autonomy, schools are being required to evaluate their own educational quality and to come up with their own plans for improvement. The responsibilities for quality assurance in education are spread across various partners. The parallel existence of these responsibilities has led the government, the educational inspectorate and schools to look for a way in which internal and external evaluations can be matched with each other. This is the subject of this contribution: how to find a balance between external and internal evaluation. The search for an appropriate balance between internal and external evaluation is underway in multiple locations and in many countries. It is to propose a scenario though we realize that specific interpretations are at present somewhat thin on the ground (Klein, 2004).

Quality Assurance: Different Responses to Differing Expectations

Quality assurance implies having an idea of what quality involves. It would therefore be inappropriate to approach this topic without first exploring what we mean by 'educational quality'. In the following section we will attempt to arrive at an operational definition of "quality". Educational Quality: a Variety of Expectations We will arrive at our interpretation of the concept of "quality" step by step. Although the following reflection might seem somewhat redundant at first sight, it will be apparent later on in this contribution that the definition of this concept is crucial to sketching out scenarios for the role of self-evaluation and school audits in a quality assurance system. Our point of departure is that: "quality means complying with expectations" (Harrington, 1994). A school can be said to be functioning optimally (in other words, to be providing good quality education) when it meets expectations. These expectations may be dictated by the government, the school board, parents, pupils and, of course, also by the school management and the teaching staff of the school itself. Examples of expectations are: raising pupil enrolment; the achievement of mathematical literacy; excellence and the guaranteeing of equal opportunities. These expectations come from both internal as well as external stakeholders. Although these are often parallel or complementary, these can also be contradictory, however. In the first instance, these expectations refer to the attainment of pre-set objectives. Quality is thus, first and foremost, meeting expectations in terms of results (i.e. effectiveness). However, effectiveness on its own does not amount to quality. How these results are reached is also of importance. It is, therefore, not possible to make a judgement about the quality of a school without taking into account the process which leads to the attainment of objectives in its entirety. Efficiency, for example, is an integral part of the expectations drawn up by the various stakeholders (i.e. value for money), but it is to be clearly distinguished from expectations in terms of results. The various stakeholders may also have clear expectations with regard to manners in the school or the didactic approach used. Expectations are often not explicitly stated. The expectations of all stakeholders must, therefore, be ascertained and discussed. Quality is thus not a characteristic of - or a task for - school management and teaching staff alone. Quality of education is something on which the government, the school board, school management, teaching staff, pupils, parents, the business world and higher education must agree by means of dialogue. Quality is related to all levels within the school and to all stakeholders (Bosker, 2002). It is not a sum total of all expectations, but rather the integration and assessment of a school-specific whole. This means that a useful definition of educational quality must, of necessity, be separated from specific content and requires an abstract description. This brings us to the following definition of quality: (Educational) quality is meeting the expectations shared by the stakeholders in an appropriate manner. The (shared) expectations are, however, of a diverse nature and with an eye on the interpretation of quality assurance it is important to make a clear distinction with regard to where these come from. We distinguish between school-internal and school-external expectations. Within the group of school-external expectations we make a further distinction between expectations which are anchored in the law and expectations which are not legally anchored. Expectations which are anchored in the law are those expectations which the government (acting on behalf of society) imposes on schools and which can be forcibly imposed. If schools fail to meet these expectations the government can- and must - take steps to sanction them.

School-external expectations which are not legally anchored derive from stakeholders whose expectations are not laid down in a legal framework. This group of stakeholders is extremely broad and growing (e.g. recipients of pupils who have successfully obtained their graduation diplomas; parents (and parents associations); pastoral services and a very wide variety of trans-national agencies such as the Organisation for Economic Co-operation and Development (OECD) and the World Bank.

These stakeholders may well make demands of schools and/or participate in decision making with regard to how educational quality is to be implemented, but they cannot act in a sanctioning manner as a government can. Finally there are school-internal expectations. These are those aspects which the school concerned places emphasis upon above and beyond the minimum requirements which are expected by society (Petegem, 1999). These expectations may, for example, be of a philosophical nature (reflecting a particular life vision) or may relate to the didactic methods used. Each type of expectation requires its own interpretation of quality assurance and of the role of self-evaluation and school audits in the quality assurance system as a whole. It is conclude that these expectations are highly diverse (Alkin, 2004).

Implications for Possible Scenarios for a Successful Combination of External and Internal Evaluation

We have demonstrated that both external and internal evaluations are necessary components of quality assurance systems. However, these cannot be combined anyway. We would now like to move on – with the attention points set out above in the back of our minds – to arrive at possible scenarios for the achievement of a successful combination of auditing and self-evaluations by schools. By rigorously applying the attention points formulated above, it would like to set out a scenario which may serve to provoke reflection. The point of departure is a distinction between two groups of school-external expectations (which may or may not be anchored in legislation) and school-internal expectations. It is also make an additional distinction between accountability and school development. In total, therefore, there are six conditions to be met when elaborating a system of quality assurance. The full implementation of this framework is an extremely complex task and it is very difficult to arrive at a consensus on this given the importance of ideological assumptions. In the following section we will focus on the role which self-evaluations, school audits and support services must play in the various domains. For each domain we will examine whether internal and external evaluations should run in parallel, sequentially or cooperatively (Kyriakides & Campbell, 2004). The domains with regard to non-legally anchored and school-internal expectations are handled together throughout, however. Our intention here is, after all, to focus primarily on the distinction between expectations - whether or not these are legally anchored. Nor are we going to explore more specific forms of self-evaluation such as formative visits by colleagues and the input of "critical friends" in self-evaluations or the specific ways in which data should assembled in conducting self-evaluations (Swaffield, 2005). This does not mean, however, that we do not subscribe to the potential of these forms of quality assurance.

Domain 1: Accountability for Legally-Anchored Expectations

In this first aspect of quality assurance we must adopt – on the basis of the arguments described above – two clear standpoints:

1. It is only in this case that an obligatory school audit must play a role; and
2. There is no room here for self-evaluation.

In essence, the inspectorate is authorized to check whether schools comply with the expectations which the government imposes upon them. From a strictly legal point of view their responsibilities are more restricted than is the case in the present situation. There should, therefore, be a 'pared down' form of school audit which is restricted to those aspects which are actually stipulated by law and which could be termed a "core audit". Core audits take place at the initiative of the government and are obligatory. The report of a core audit is first and foremost summative and limited, as standard, to those aspects which are imposed on schools by the government. This does not mean, of course, that the audit may not look at other processes in the school, but this is done as a means to an end and not as an objective per se. After all, it is not possible to talk about the quality of a product without acquiring an understanding of how that product is created.

The validity and reliability of self-evaluations is insufficiently guaranteed in the event of an obligatory summative evaluation. This means, therefore, that self-evaluation as such does not have a role to play in this first aspect of quality assurance. In this domain conducting self-evaluations as a preparation to (core) school audits is thus not an appropriate method. The reverse may be possible, however: the results of a core audit may provide useful information which could then be included in a self-evaluation. In this case, we find ourselves in the second domain of quality assurance.

Domain 2: School Development with Regard to Legally-Anchored Expectations

The legally-anchored expectations which schools are obliged to meet can also be the subject of school development. This is because in many cases the objectives imposed by the government are also shared by schools and also because schools are themselves aware of the importance of complying with these expectations. In these school development processes a role may be assigned to the core audit report, for the educational support services and for self-evaluation. A central element in this domain of quality assurance is self-evaluations by school focused on the extent to which the school concerned complies with the expectations of the government. The initiative for undertaking such a self-evaluation ought preferably to be taken by the school or a supporting body and not by the government as monitoring party. The aim of this self evaluation is thus also formative and focused on development. Schools want to describe and evaluate their own functioning with respect to legal expectations with an eye to taking decisions or undertaking initiatives which make it possible to respond (even) better to these expectations. In principle, self-evaluations in this domain can be independent of the core audit, but they can also be combined. Possible objectives of self-evaluations with legal expectations as their focus are anticipating, analysing and discussing the findings of a core audit and establishing suitable implementation methods. In this sense, the core audit report also has an important informative value in this domain of quality assurance.

This report must not only contain findings with regard to the expectations investigated, but must also indicate how obstacles observed can best be tackled in the opinion of the educational inspectorate. There must, therefore, be a proper follow-up to the core audit, although ideally this ought not to be carried out by the inspectorate itself. The inspectorate writes its report and explains its content and this is where its role ends. Once the audit has been completed, the educational support services must be closely involved in what follows in order to guarantee the formative role of the evaluation. Another important element here is the creation of formative (external) evaluation moments which are independent of the core audit.

The time interval between (core) audits is at present too great to permit them to play a systematic role in the process of school development. Yet school development is a continuing process. Initiatives need to be taken, therefore, to make contact with schools in a formative manner with an eye to establishing their strengths and weaknesses in relation to compliance with legal expectations. In the first instance, the supervision services have an important role to play in this.

Domains 3 and 5: Accountability of Non-Legally Anchored and School-internal Expectations

In principle, schools do not have to render account to the government with regard to external expectations which are not legally-anchored, but they may do this directly or indirectly to those bodies and (groups) of people who originally formulated these expectations. The same applies to school-internal expectations. In both these domains of quality assurance it is essentially a matter of opening communication between schools and the persons and groups concerned. According to own research, schools are currently somewhat closed. How and to whom account ought to be rendered are questions which have yet to be clarified, however. This is a social discussion which has yet to get under way in Flanders. This makes it particularly difficult to determine at present what roles could be allotted to self-evaluation and school audits in quality assurance as a whole. Both are means to an end which can only be employed once a clear aim has been identified. A determining factor is, for example, the role to be given to the government (or its inspectorate) in guaranteeing this form of accountability.

Domains 4 and 6: School Development with Regard to Non-Legally Anchored and School-internal Expectations

School development is concerned with much more than merely the "minimum" which the inspectors come to audit. The non-legally anchored and school-internal expectations ought also to be part of this. It is in the first instance up to the school itself to describe and evaluate its own functioning through cycles of self-evaluation. The context-related nature of the non-legally anchored and school-internal expectations makes it difficult to establish general frameworks, of course. Yet this does not mean that external evaluations cannot have a scope-broadening, encouraging and legitimizing impact on self-evaluation activities. In these domains of quality assurance there can thus also be a role for external evaluations by the educational inspectorate and supervisory services. At present, schools do not have to render account to the inspectorate with regard to expectations in these domains. That said, however, the audits of the inspectorate can play a valuable role. In the course of the core audit, the inspectorate does, after all, collect data with regard to aspects which go beyond the merely legal. We have commented above that the report of the core audit in this scenario restricts itself to those aspects which the government stipulates for schools. At the request of the school other aspects of the functioning of the school could also be included in a supplement to the core audit report. This section of the audit report would have a purely formative function and the inspectorate would then give its opinion on aspects which form part of the audit, at the request of schools It must be possible for the inspectorate - at the request of and in consultation with the school - to shine its expert light on part of the route travelled in the direction which the school wishes to go. A further step might also be taken here. At the request of the school under inspection, the inspectorate could expand the summative core audit by including formative theme audits. These (non-obligatory) theme audits focus on aspects which go beyond the legal expectations per se, such as the pedagogical/didactic policy of the school, or its policy implementation capacity. On the initiative of the school the contents of the core audit could be supplemented with some form of external formative evaluation.

Educational support services also have a role to play here. It is in the first instance up to them to provide schools with formative evaluation moments regarding expectations which exceed the purely legal. Schools must be able to turn to the supervisory service for support both in terms of content and with regard to methodology. This might take a wide variety of useful forms: providing additional training; the supervision of self-evaluations; making tools and methods available; setting up partnerships between schools which participate in self-evaluation and arranging exchanges of formative visits around a joint framework; establishing forms of audits, etc.

The specific implementation of the role of self-evaluation and school audits as part of an overall quality assurance system is no easy matter. Educational policy-makers in various countries across the globe are currently struggling with this problem. Questioning existing practices and looking for possible alternatives often seems only to leave us with yet more questions. This is a necessary process, however, if we are to create a comprehensive and better-functioning quality assurance system. In this connection it is important to arrive at a shared vision with regard to what the objectives of such a system ought to be. Only when these objectives are clear, will we be in a position to clarify the respective roles which self evaluations and school audits can play in quality assurance as a whole (Kyriakides & Campbell, 2004). Fundamental reflections are thus crucially important in relation to the quality assurance system. In attempting to arrive at a possible scenario, we have very strongly emphasized the difference between formative and summative forms of evaluation.

Conclusion

The initiative for school development always lies with the school itself. Unless schools specifically request this, the inspectorate should, in this scenario, limit itself to its core tasks. The inspectors must conduct a two track policy - strictly and transparently: an accountability-orientated policy track; and a development-orientated policy track. In addition to this, possibilities must be created - or further expanded - so that schools can call on external actors in order to ensure the quality of internal evaluation. This contribution contains material for reflection. We have set out arguments both for and against an integration of self-evaluations and school audits in the rendering of account and the development of schools. In order to make the implications of these arguments more specific we have developed a possible scenario. Although we are favourably inclined towards the logic behind this scenario it is not our intention to provide definite answers. Our purpose in setting out this scenario is to formulate critical reflections in connection with existing quality assurance systems and to offer suggestions for possible alternatives. First and foremost our intention was to question a number of assumptions as these assumptions stand in the way of the critical examination of the present quality assurance system which is so desperately needed.

REFERENCES

1. Alkin, M.C. (Ed.). (2004). *Evaluation Roots. Tracing Theorists' Views and Influences.* Sage, London.
2. Kyriakides, L., & Campbell, R.J. (2004). *School Self-Evaluation and School Improvement: A Critique of Landscape of Education Policy.* Studies in Educational Evaluation 34, 173-179.
3. Swaffield, S., & MacBeath, J. (2005). *School Self-evaluation and the Role of a Critical Friend.* Cambridge.
4. Thamarasseri, Ismail. (2012). *Essentials of Educational Evaluation.* New Delhi: Kanishka Publishers.

9 Educational Measurement for Maximise Student Learning

Introduction

Measurement refers to the process by which the attributes or dimensions of some physical object are determined. One exception seems to be in the use of the word measure in determining the IQ of a person. The phrase, "this test measures IQ" is commonly used. Measuring such things as attitudes or preferences also applies. However, when we measure, we generally use some standard instrument to determine how big, tall, heavy, voluminous, hot, cold, fast, or straight something actually is. Standard instruments refer to instruments such as rulers, scales, thermometers, pressure gauges, etc. We measure to obtain information about what is. Such information may or may not be useful, depending on the accuracy of the instruments we use, and our skill at using them. There are few such instruments in the social sciences that approach the validity and reliability of say a 15 cm ruler/scale. We measure how big a classroom is in terms of square feet, we measure the temperature of the room by using a thermometer, and we use Ohm meters to determine the voltage, amperage, and resistance in a circuit. In all of these examples, we are not assessing anything; we are simply collecting information relative to some established rule or standard. Assessment is therefore quite different from measurement, and has uses that suggest very different purposes.

Measurement often connotes a broader concept in comparison to test. We can measure characteristics in ways other than by giving tests. Using observations, rating scales or any other device that allows us to obtain information in a quantitative form is measurement. Gronlund (1985) defined measurement as "the process of obtaining numerical description of the degree to which an individual possesses a particular characteristic".

Generally, measurement is the process by which we ascertain the quantity of a thing. It is the assignment of a numerical index to the thing we assess. In measurement we compare a known quantity (for instance; maximum mark 100) with an unknown quantity to get information about the unknown quantity. For example; Mr. Dinesh Kumar got 84 mark out of 100 in his course.

Educational measurement refers to the use of educational assessments and the analysis of data such as scores obtained from educational assessments to infer the abilities and proficiencies of students. The approaches overlap with those in psychometrics. Educational measurement is the assigning of numerals to traits such as achievement, interest, attitudes, aptitudes, intelligence and performance.

The aim of theory and practice in educational measurement is typically to measure abilities and levels of attainment by students in areas such as reading, writing, mathematics, science and so forth. Traditionally, attention focuses on whether assessments are reliable and valid. In practice, educational measurement is largely concerned with the analysis of data from educational assessments or tests. Typically, this means using total scores on assessments, whether they are multiple choice or open-ended and marked using marking rubrics or guides.

In technical terms, the pattern of scores by individual students to individual items is used to infer so-called scale locations of students, the "measurements". This process is one form of scaling. Essentially, higher total scores give higher scale locations, consistent with the traditional and everyday use of total scores. If certain theory is used, though, there is not a strict correspondence between the ordering of total scores and the ordering of scale locations.

In terms of the broad body of purely mathematical theory drawn on, there is substantial overlap between educational measurement and psychometrics. One of the aims of applying theory and techniques in educational measurement is to try to place the results of different tests administered to different groups of students on a single or common scale through processes known as test equating. The rationale is that because different assessments usually have different difficulties, the total scores cannot be directly compared. The aim of trying to place results on a common scale is to allow comparison of the scale locations inferred from the totals via scaling processes.

The process of measurement as it implies involves carrying out actual measurement in order to assign a quantitative meaning to a quality i.e. what is the length of the chalkboard? Determining this must be physically done. Measurement is therefore a process of assigning numerals to objects, quantities or events in other to give quantitative meaning to such qualities. In the classroom, to determine a child's performance, you need to obtain quantitative measures on the individual scores of the child. If the child scores 80 in Mathematics, there is no other interpretation you should give it. You cannot say he has passed or failed. Measurement stops at ascribing the quantity but not making value judgement on the child's performance. In short, Measurement is the process by which we ascertain the quantity of a thing. It is the assignment of a numerical index to the thing we assess. For Example, Mr. John Babu got 70 marks in test paper. Doesn't mean that he is clever in Maths. The score 70 is simply a measurement of his achievement in Maths.

- "Measurement is the process of assigning symbols to dimensions of phenomena in order to characterise the status of a phenomena as precisely as possible" - *M. Brad field.*
- "Measurement is defined as the assignment of one of a set of numbers to each of a set of persons or objects according to certain established rules. The set of numbers depends up on the nature of the characteristics being measured and up on the type of measuring instrument used" - *Prof. Richard. H. Lideman.*

Measurement process is conceptually simple. The only requirements are a set of objects, a set of quantitative numbers, and possibly a rule for the assignment of a number to each objects. Evaluation is perhaps the most complex and least understood of the terms. Inherent in the idea of evaluation is "value." When we evaluate, what we are doing is engaging in some process that is designed to provide information that will help us make a judgment about a given situation. Generally, any evaluation process requires information about the situation in question. A situation is an umbrella term that takes into account such ideas as objectives, goals, standards, procedures, and so on. When we evaluate, we are saying that the process will yield information regarding the worthiness, appropriateness, goodness, validity, legality, etc., of something for which a reliable measurement or assessment has been made. Teachers, in particular, are constantly evaluating students, and such evaluations are usually done in the context of comparisons between what was intended (learning, progress, behaviour) and what was obtained. Evaluation is a "process that allows one to make a judgment about the desirability or value of a measure".

For example Ms. Jasmine got 95 mark out of 100 in Sociology.	It is measurement
Teacher says, she is excellent in Sociology.	It is a evaluation.

Gronlund (1970) defines "Evaluation as the systematic process of collecting, analysing and interpreting information to determine the extent of which the objectives are being attained". Tylor (1950) defines evaluation as "the process of determining to what extent the educational objectives are being realized".

Characteristics of Evaluation

- Evaluation is a continuous process.
- Evaluation includes academic and non academic subjects.
- Evaluation is the procedure for improving the product.
- Discovering needs of an individual and designing learning experiences.
- Evaluation provides quality control at every stage of the teaching-learning process.
- Evaluation is function of learner and teacher.
- Good evaluation is one which is done by the teacher, of the taught as an individual.

To sum up, we measure distance, we assess learning, and we evaluate results in terms of some set of criteria. These three terms are certainly connected, but it is useful to think of them as separate but connected ideas and processes.

Difference between Measurement and Evaluation

The main difference Between measurement and evaluation explained with the help of following examples.

- A teacher measures Mr. Saleem's height to be 180 cm. The teacher evaluates his height when he says that he is long.
- A teacher measures Miss. Ranjini's achievement in Economics to be 50% he evaluates her achievement when he says that Ms. Ranjini's achievement in Economics is satisfactory.

The major differences between Evaluation and Measurement are shown in Table 9.1 as follows:

Table 9.1

Measurement versus Evaluation

Measurement	Evaluation
It is the process of ascertaining the extent the value of something or quantity of something.	It is the process of determining
The scope is narrow	The scope is wide
Quantitative	Qualitative, Judgment of values.
It refers only "how much" without any reference to purpose, past or future. It only concerned the present.	It refers to "how good" with reference to purpose, present, past and future.
Measurement is objective and impersonal. It doesn't change with change of individuals.	Subjective and personal to a great extent.

(Table Contd...)

Measurement	Evaluation
Precise and scientific. Scope of measurement is limited.	Interpretive and Philosophical.
Not a continues process. It is occasional. Tests are conducted only occasionally to get a measure of pupils achievement.	Evaluation is a continuous process. Teachers are evaluation the pupils ever and soon.
Measurement is independent of Evaluation.	Correct evaluation depended up on correct measurement.
Correct evaluation depended up on correct measurement.	Scope of evaluation is unlimited.

Evaluation has a wider meaning. It goes beyond measurement. When from useful information including measurement, we make a judgement, that is evaluation. Example: The teacher may evaluate the student Ms. Geetha that she is doing well in mathematics, because most of the class scored 50/100. This is an example of evaluation using quantitative data (measurable information). The teacher might also make an evaluation based on qualitative data, such as her observations that Ms. Geetha works hard, has an enthusiastic attitude towards mathematics and finishes her assignments quickly.

- Evaluation is a Science of providing information for decision making.
- It Includes measurement, assessment and testing.
- It is a process that involves.
- Information gathering.
- Information processing.
- Judgement forming.
- Decision making.

From the above, we can arrive at the following concept of evaluation.

- Evaluation is a concept that has emerged as a prominent process of assessing, testing and measuring. Its main objective is Qualitative Improvement.
- Evaluation is a process of making value judgements over a level of performance or achievement. Making value judgements in Evaluation process presupposes the set of objectives.
- Evaluation implies a critical assessment of educative process and its outcome in the light of the objectives.

Evaluation is the process by which we judge the value of a thing. It is the process of determining the extent to which an educational objective attained. It is something more than measurement. In order to judge the performance of students in a calss test, we seek more information such as:

- "How many pupils took that test?
- Which is the highest score?
- Which is the lowest mark?
- What is the class average?

James. M. Brad says, "Evaluation is the assignment of symbols to phenomenon in order to characterise the worth or value of a phenomenon, usually with reference to some social, cultural or scientific standards". For the purpose of schematic representation, the three concepts of evaluation, measurement and testing have traditionally been demonstrated in three concentric circles of varying sizes. This is what Lynch (2001) has followed in depicting the relationship among these concepts.

Purposes of Evaluation

- Evaluation is the process of determining the extent to which the objectives are achieved.
- It is Concerned not only with the appraisal of achievement, but also with its improvement.
- Evaluation is a continuous and a dynamic process. Evaluation helps in forming the following decisions.

What should teachers learn about evaluation?

- Choosing evaluation methods appropriate for instructional decisions;
- Developing methods appropriate for instructional decisions;
- Administering, scoring and interpreting the results of both externally produced and teacher-produced evaluation methods;
- Using evaluation results when making decisions about individual students, planning teaching, developing curriculum and school improvement;
- Developing valid pupil grading procedures, which use pupil assessments;
- Communicating evaluation results to students, parents, other lay audiences, and other educators;
- Recognizing unethical, illegal and otherwise inappropriate evaluation methods and uses of evaluation information.

Assessment is a process by which information is obtained relative to some known objective or goal. Assessment is a broad term that includes testing. A test is a special form of assessment. Tests are assessments made under contrived circumstances especially so that they may be administered. In other words, all tests are assessments, but not all assessments are tests. We test at the end of a lesson or unit. We assess progress at the end of a school year through testing. Whether implicit or explicit, assessment is most usefully connected to some goal or objective for which the assessment is designed. A test or assessment yields information relative to an objective or goal. In that sense, we test or assess to determine whether or not an objective or goal has been obtained. Assessment of skill attainment is rather straightforward. Either the skill exists at some acceptable level or it doesn't. Skills are readily demonstrable.

Assessment of understanding is much more difficult and complex. Skills can be practiced; understandings cannot. We can assess a person's knowledge in a variety of ways, but there is always a hurdle, an inference that we make about what a person does in relation to what it signifies about what he knows.

To many teachers (and students), "assessment" simply means giving students tests and assigning them grades. This conception of assessment is not only limited, but also limiting. It fails to take into account both the utility of assessment and its importance in the teaching/learning process. In the most general sense, assessment is the process of making a judgment or measurement of worth of an entity (e.g., person, process, or programme). Educational assessment involves gathering and evaluating data evolving from planned learning activities or programmes. This form of assessment is often referred to as evaluation. Learner assessment represents a particular type of educational assessment normally conducted by teachers and designed to serve several related purpose. These purposed include:

- motivating and directing learning;
- providing feedback to student on their performance;
- providing feedback on instruction and/or the curriculum; and
- ensuring standards of progression are met.

Learner assessment is best conceived as a form of two-way communication in which feedback on the educational process or product is provided to its key stakeholders. Specifically, learner assessment involves communication to teachers (feedback on teaching); students (feedback on learning); curriculum designers (feedback on curriculum) and administrators (feedback on use of resources). For teachers and curriculum/course designers, carefully constructed learner assessment techniques can help determining whether or not the stated goals are being achieved. Classroom assessment can help teachers answer the following specific questions:

- To what extent are my students achieving the stated goals?
- How should I allocate class time for the current topic?
- Can I teach this topic in a more efficient or effective way?
- What parts of this course/unit are my students finding most valuable?

- How will I change this course/unit the next time I teach it?
- Which grades do I assign my students?

For students, learner assessment answers a different set of questions:

- Do I know what my instructor thinks is most important?
- Am I mastering the course content?
- How can I improve the way I study in this course?
- What grade am I earning in this course?

Assessment versus Evaluation: Depending on the authority or dictionary consulted, assessment and evaluation may be treated as synonyms or as distinctly different concepts. As noted above, if a distinction exists, it probably involves what is being measured and why and how the measurements are made. In terms of what, it is often said that we assess students and we evaluate instruction. This distinction derives from the use of evaluation research methods to make judgments about the worth of educational activities. Moreover, it emphasizes an individual focus of assessment, i.e., using information to help identify a learner's needs and document his or her progress toward meeting goals.

In terms of why and how the measurements are made, the following table 9.2 compares and contrasts assessment and evaluation on several important dimension, some of which were previously defined.

Table 9.2

Assessment versus Evaluation

Dimension	Assessment	Evaluation
Timing	Formative	Summative
Focus of Measurement	Process-Oriented	Product-Oriented
Relationship Between Teacher and Student	Reflective	Prescriptive
Findings and Uses	Diagnostic	Judgmental
Modifiability of Criteria, Measures	Flexible	Fixed
Standards of Measurement	Absolute(Individual)	Comparative
Relation Between Objects of Assessment and Evaluation	Cooperative	Competitive

Adapted from Apple, D.K. & Krumsieg, K. (1998). *Process Education Teaching Institute Handbook.* Pacific Crest.

Why is Assessment Important?

Hopefully by this point in your life you have discovered that learning can be fun! You have probably also realized that you are constantly learning, whether you are in a classroom, a car, or a kitchen.

Assessment helps you Build Confidence in your Ability to Learn

Perhaps you have heard that the global work culture is changing. Unlike your grandfather, you will probably have a number of different jobs and careers during your lifetime. In order to be successful, you will need to have confidence in your ability to learn and you will need to become a lifelong learner. Assessment plays a key role in developing your confidence in your ability to learn, as well as in developing your lifelong learning skills.

The definitions for each are:

- **Test:** A method to determine a student's ability to complete certain tasks or demonstrate mastery of a skill or knowledge of content. Some types would be multiple choice tests, or a weekly spelling test. While it is commonly used interchangeably with assessment, or even evaluation, it can be distinguished by the fact that a test is one form of an assessment.
- **Measurement**, refers to the set of procedures and the principles for how to use the procedures in educational tests and assessments. Some of the basic principles of measurement in educational evaluations would be raw scores, percentile ranks, derived scores, standard scores, etc.
- **Evaluation:** Procedures used to determine whether the student meets a preset criteria, such as qualifying for special education services. This uses assessment (remember that an assessment may be a test) to make a determination of qualification in accordance with a predetermined criteria.
- **Assessment:** The process of gathering information to monitor progress and make educational decisions if necessary. An assessment may include a test, but also includes methods such as observations, interviews, behaviour monitoring, etc.

Assessment versus Grading

Based on the above discussion, grading could be considered a component of assessment, i.e., a formal, summative, final and product-oriented judgment of overall quality of worth of a student's performance or achievement in a particular educational activity, e.g., a course. Generally, grading also employs a comparative standard of measurement and sets up a competitive relationship between those receiving the grades. Most proponents of assessment, however, would argue that grading and assessment are two different things, or at least opposite pole on the evaluation spectrum. For them, assessment measures student growth and progress on an individual basis, emphasizing informal, formative, process oriented reflective feedback and communication between student and teacher.

Conclusion

When defined within an educational setting, assessment, evaluation, and testing are all used to measure how much of the assigned materials students are mastering, how well student are learning the materials, and how well student are meeting the stated goals and objectives. Although you may believe that assessments only provide instructors with information on which to base a score or grade, assessments also help you to assess your own learning. Education professionals make distinctions between assessment, evaluation, and testing. However, for the purposes of this tutorial, all you really need to understand is that these are three different terms for referring to the process of figuring out how much you know about a given topic and that each term has a different meaning. To simplify things, we will use the term "assessment" throughout this tutorial to refer to this process of measuring what you know and have learned. A test or quiz is used to examine someone's knowledge of something to determine what he or she knows or has learned. Testing measures the level of skill or knowledge that has been reached. Evaluation is the process of making judgments based on criteria and evidence. Assessment is the process of documenting knowledge, skills, attitudes and beliefs, usually in measurable terms. The goal of assessment is to make improvements, as opposed to simply being judged. In an educational context, assessment is the process of describing, collecting, recording, scoring, and interpreting information about learning.

REFERENCES

1. *Assessment versus Evaluation*. retrieved on 05-03-2016 from http://www.pcrest2.com/LO/assessment/3a.htm
2. Concept of Evaluation and its Principles. retrieved on 05-03-2016 from http://wikieducator.org/CONCEPT_OF_EVALUATION_AND_ITS_PRINCIPLES
3. *Differences between Testing, Assessment, and Evaluation*. retrieved on 05-03-2016 from http://tutorials.istudy.psu.edu/testing/testing2.html
4. *Educational measurement*. retrieved on 05-03-2016 from https://en.wikipedia.org/wiki/Educational_measurement
5. Farooq, U. (2013). *Difference between Measurement and Evaluation*. retrieved on 04-03-2016 from http://www.studylecturenotes.com/social-sciences/education/419-difference-between-measurement-and-evaluation-with-examples
6. Graph Pad Software, Inc. (2019). *What is the Difference between Ordinal, Interval and Ratio Variables?* Retrieved on 05-03-2016 from http://www.graphpad.com/support/faqid/1089/
7. http://oer.avu.org/bitstream/handle/123456789/78/Educational%20Evaluation%20and%20Testing.pdf?sequence=1
8. Kalanilayam, S. (2007). *Measurement and Evaluation*. retrieved on 05-03-2016 from http://sathitech.blogspot.in/2007/11/measurement-and-evaluation.html
9. Kizlik, B. (2012). *Measurement, Assessment, and Evaluation in Education*. retrieved on 04-03-2016 from http://drjj.uitm.edu.my/DRJJ/OBE%20FSG%20Dec07/OBEJan2010/DrJJ-Measure-assess-evaluate-ADPRIMA-n-more-17052012.pdf

10. Lynch, B.K. (2001). Rethinking Assessment from a Critical Perspective. *Language Testing* 18 (4) 351-372.
11. *Measurement and Evaluation in Education*. Retrieved on 04-03-2016 from http://www.dphu.org/uploads/attachements/books/books_4737_0.pdf
12. *Measurement and Evaluation*. Retrieved on 05-03-2016 from https://polguart.wordpress.com/2010/03/17/module-1-measurement-and-evaluation/
13. St.Ann's College of Education (2012). *The B.Ed. Aid*. Retrieved on 04-03-2016 from http://thebedaid.blogspot.in/2012/02/difference-between-evaluation-and.html
14. *Test (Assessment)*. Retrieved on 05-03-2016 from https://en.wikipedia.org/wiki/Test_(assessment)
15. Thamarasseri, Ismail. (2012). *Essentials of Educational Evaluation*. New Delhi: Kanishka Publishers.
16. Thamarasseri, Ismail. (2012). *Teaching of Social Science for the 21st Century*. New Delhi: Kanishka Publishers.
17. Thamarasseri, Ismail. (2012). *Trends and Developments in Social Science Education*. New Delhi: Kanishka Publishers.

10 Developing an Institutional Plan

Introduction

An institutional plan is a programme of development and improvement prepared by an educational institution on the basis of its felt needs and the resources available or likely to be made available. Institutional planning is a programme with a view to improving institutional programme and institutional practices, constitutes a plan for and institution. It is based on the principle of optimum utilization of the resources available in the school and the community. The plan may be for a longer duration or a shorter duration. Institutional planning provides a direction to qualitative development of an institution in various manifestations. Effective management, efficient coordination and successful evaluation would help in developing better institutions of higher education. The purpose is to align academic priorities with financial and capital resources in order to ensure the responsible use of all resources. The purpose is also to translate the educational ideal into architectural expression at institutes of higher learning. It is a serious team work which requires team spirit and to ensure participation from all stakeholders including teachers, administration, experts, analysts ... so as to understand the new opportunities, realities and challenges. This chapter gives a meta narrative on institutional planning and a highlight to the several vital aspects institutional planning.

Speaking at the at the tenth convocation of Mizoram University President of India, Shri. Pranab Mukherjee said, "A higher educational institution is a role-model for the society. It must leverage all expertise to contribute to the socio-economic development of the region. Education supports two fundamental objectives of human existence: proliferation of knowledge and formation of character. Higher education especially has a unique role to play in preparing the torch-bearers of tomorrow who will endeavour in different fields".

The higher education systems in developing countries are under great strain. They are chronically underfunded, but face escalating demand - approximately half of today's higher education students live in the developing world. Faculty are often under qualified, lack motivation, are poorly rewarded. Students are poorly taught and curricula underdeveloped. There are notable exceptions, but currently, across most of the developing countries, the potential of higher education to promote development is being realized only marginally.

The Working Party Report of the UNESCO (1963) quoted, "... institutional planning is not an isolated activity, it must be undertaken in the framework of comprehensive development planning, and must be viewed in the larger context of all the steps required for effective educational development." The question of quality cannot be neglected; therefore a collaborative effort amongst political leaders, academicians and practitioners is required. In a developing country like India with basic dire needs of water, electricity, housing, employment ... a practical blue print and a working plan is required. This working plan should address the data based needs and academic issues, in short, it should be prepared on the basis of felt needs of future and resources available or likely to be available with a view to improving institutional practices".

The characteristics or requisites of a good institutional plan is that, it should be need based and not grant based. Institutional plan will ensure the optimum utilization of resources in a co-operative and goal oriented manner. It should be a prospective, specific, student centred, scientific and task oriented. It is to be helpful to improve the motivation and work culture among all stake holders, continuous institutional improvement and development in collaboration with the community with a democratic outlook. Inspection and monitoring is one of the component of institutional planning; so that we can eliminate wastage of money and losing of precious time.

Institutional planning is a unique answer to four issues. viz.,

- Giving freedom to teacher
- Making teaching effective
- Involving every teacher in formulation and implementation of planning
- Effective work by monitoring resources

Modern education, particularly higher education is confronted with three major challenges viz. *excellence, equity* and *efficiency* of the systems. Our major concerns while planning should be maintenance of quality, equalization of educational opportunity, improvements of efficiency and effectiveness in the system of higher education.

Need and Importance of Institutional Planning

The Education Commission (1964-66) has aptly said, "no comprehensive programme of educational development can ever be put across unless it involves every educational institution and all the human factors connected with its teachers, students and the local community and unless it provides the necessary inducements to put in their best efforts." Both quantitative and qualitative improvement of education is aimed at through institutional planning. All concerned teachers, students, community and the public are involved in the planning process meant for development of an institution.

- **For betterment and improvement:** All institutions have some plans. All the heads of institutions make plans and each teacher also plans. In fact each head and teacher does plan but this planning may not be systematic adequate and clear. This planning may not exist in a definite or regular form. Planning may mostly be routine planning of the curriculum, syllabus, time table and examination etc. and it may not exist in a definite or regular form and it may be repeated from term to term and from session to session without much thinking.
- **To give proper direction to educational objectives:** Institutional planning will give you right direction to the educational planning in the country i.e., the upward direction from bottom to top. In the normal trend followed today the direction of planning is from top to bottom. Institutional planning is the recognition of the role of administrators, teachers, parents, students, educationists and social reformers in the process of planning of education in the country.
- **For maximum utilization of resources:** Institutional planning leads to optimum use of the existing resources. As a nation we face a great scarcity of resources with increasing needs and demands from every quarter. Therefore we must plan for maximum utilization of scarce resource.
- **For national development:** Educational planning must fit into the overall national planning for developmental purposes. As such it gets importance from the need for collective efforts of the people. The implementation of plans and programmes is as important and vital as plan formulation. Institutional planning has a special contribution to make in national development.
- **To encourage initiative of individual teacher:** Institutional plan encourages initiative freedom and creativity of the teacher makes the individual teacher effective. It motivates them too strive harder for achieving excellence. It draws out the best of the teachers.

- **For democratization of planning:** Institutional planning democratizes the process of planning because it takes into confidence the students the teachers the parents and the head of the institution. J.P. Naik says, "A major reform, I propose, therefore is that the planning that resembles an inverted pyramid should be broad-based and decentralized by introducing the system of institutional plans." He strongly planned to have a fine blend of the centralized and decentralized systems of educational planning in our country.

Essentials of Institutional Planning

There are different level of improvement programmes are there. The head of the institution should realize that all improvement programmers will not go at the same rate. Some programmes will develop at a faster take than others. For example; in the case of a newly started university, the establishment and infrastructure enhancement should be in a speed track. While planning for the institution the experience of the past year should be taken into consideration and the plan should be a forward looking plan aiming at high ideal, viz. too be the pursuit of excellence. The Head should not frame the institutional planning in isolation of the perspective plan, national plan and state plan. Main target of the national plan should be squarely put before the staff member to give them direction for planning. The objectives of Institutional Planning are:

- Instruction or the teaching learning process is to be improved.
- Infrastructural facilities need be developed. Improvement of library equipment and facilities in institution
- Optimum utilization of all kinds of existing resources - material, human
- Community and local resources must be utilized for improving the institutions.
- Local talents and expertise need be harnessed fully. Providing an opportunity to the local community, school staff and student to join hands and improve the institution
- Harnessing community resources and goodwill to improve and develop the institution.
- All kinds of co-curricular activities need be organized. Developing co-curricular programmes in the institution like extension activities, social service and adult educational programmes, and youth service which will make the institution as a community centre.

The advantages of institutional planning:

- Institutional planning is realistic and need based. In the past, planning was done for an area or an institution from a distance without relating it to the actual needs.

- It is economic and cost effective. Because while planning, the available resources are taken into account and locally available materials are likely to be utilized. The programmes which are beneficial to a large majority are planned and executed, so these are cost effective.
- Institutional planning gives scope for large participation. The persons who matter and those who are affected are consulted and involved from the very beginning. That is why it is participatory and democratic.
- Since, it is a grass root planning, it gives psychological satisfaction of sharing and belongingness, which contributes to success in implementation.
- Institutional planning is flexible and dynamic. As it is locally planned, changes can be done easily in response to local needs and demands.
- It is freedom oriented and initiative based. Teachers, students and parents are at liberty to plan and implement the programmes which they feel useful and practicable.

Role of teacher in Institutional Planning: Generally in higher education sector the teachers are not in the part and parcel of institutional planning. They putting this ball to administrators court. But it is related to different aspects of an institution - academic, administrative and financial, short term and long term. Hence it becomes comprehensive, more practical and feasible. Teachers can play a crucial role in institutional planning. The role of teachers in institutional planning can be summed up under the following points:

- **Identification of needs:** An institutional plan should be based on the needs of the educational institution. Teachers should play an important role in identifying these needs. They should help in making a thorough survey of the college or university in order to find out the problems. They can discuss pros and cons of the problems in staff meetings. They can analyse the present position in respects of various needs of the institution like adequacy of school building, furniture and equipment library and laboratory facilities admission procedure, enrolment of students and system of examination.
- **Survey of resources:** Teachers should play a vital role in making a survey of the existing Resources available in the institution, resources easily available through the Government, Management and any other funding bodies. The can also review the resources available in the community like public library, playground, bank,

factories, industries workshops, hospitals etc. Teachers should play active role in making the best use of these resources for the benefits of the students.

- **Preparation of improvement programmes:** Teachers should help the head of the institution in preparing a list of improvement programmes for the institution with details about each programmer. S/he should help the head of the institution in defining each improvement programme in terms of utility for the school involvement of school population and evaluation and follow up. S/he can play a significant role in starting improvement programmes projects and action research investigations.
- **Implementing the project:** Teacher makes a selection of the projects that are to be undertaken and guidelines are prepared. The projects should be executed through the material and human resources at command. The execution will be done through the co-operation of teacher and other personals like headmaster students and members of the community.

Institutional Planning – Steps: Institutional planning should be comprehensive and should embrace the whole educational system with all aspects of institutional life. It should be integrated with the plans and programmes of broad economic and social development. The major steps of institutional planning are:

- Identifying the needs of the institution
- Pooling together the resources available
- Preparing a plan of action
- Implementing the plan
- Evaluating and taking corrective actions.

Institutional plant: The term institutional plant includes the site, building, furniture and equipment. There are some criteria to be observed in selecting a institutional site. it should be within the easy reach of the pupils, it should have public transportation facilities, it should not be too near to bus stand, railway station, factories, cinema theatres, liquor shops or cremation grounds, it should be free from disturbing noises, it should be located in a healthy environment, it should provide safe and healthy conditions to the pupils and it should be sufficient to meet all the educational requirements of the students, including playground.

The building of the institution should be beautiful and strong, it should meet all the educational requirements, it must provide all facilities for curricular and co-curricular activities, it should be safeguard the health and safety of the pupils and teachers, each unit of the institution building should be designed to suit the purpose, but it should have a satisfactory co-ordination with other units and it should be adaptable to the changing requirements of education. Apart from the regular class rooms there should be special rooms for lab, store room for science equipments and materials, libraries, a school hall, teachers' room, head's room, office room, dining hall, waiting room for girls, visitors room, auditorium, toilets etc. While planning, rooms for special subjects should be located close to each other; viz., Science room and laboratory should be adjacent, Library in central place, Heads/Dean room should be so placed that he could have an overall view of the whole school campus from his/her room. While planning class rooms the size of the class, lighting, ventilation, the place of writing board, fixing projectors etc should be checked.

Lack of good furniture might result in poor postures of students, which in turn can affect their health, efficiency and even attitude. The seats and other furniture should suit the age and body measurement of pupils. While arranging the furniture the following points must be in mind; The desks should be arranged at right angles to the window walls, each student should be allowed at least 45 centimetres of space with enough moving space in between group of desks, and between desk and walls, the teacher must be able to move freely among these in order to give individual attention to pupils, there should not be more than six rows of desks, there should be sufficient writing boards in each class room and there should be shelves for keeping the books and for storing equipments.

Rabindra Nath Tagore said; "A good library is one that keeps books on every subject – but selected books; where the librarian is a true devotee, devote of ulterior seeking, from pride in the mere loading of shelves, capable of discriminating rejection". Library is the store house of books and no system of higher education can succeed without a well stocked library. The efficient running of the library depends upon the factors - role of librarian, role of teachers, location of the library room, quality of books. The books for the library should be selected with reference to the educational needs, vocational needs and recreational needs of the students. Reference books and encyclopaedias should be readily made available for teachers and pupils. There should be a library supply of online and print periodicals and newspapers, which would be useful to students and teachers.

Laboratory provides help in making activity dominated teaching more successful and interest is created in the subjects of study. In addition to a big room where experiments are performed, a lecture hall and a store room also be provided. The size of their rooms should be determined according to the number of students, so that at least 3 square meters of space is available for work of each student. There should be a well-equipped office in schools/departments in order to ensure effective administration of the school/department/centres. The office room should have filing cabinets and racks for keeping files in orderly manner. Steel almirahs for keeping confidential papers also necessary. Maintenance of different records is very important for institutional administration.

Experience has shown that achieving all-round development of the learner is not possible with curricular activities alone. The pupils have to provide with certain dynamic activities meant for all round development of the learner is called co-curricular activities. Co-curricular activities are not directly part of the regular studies in the class rooms but at the same time they supplement the curricular experience. While framing institutional planning this also need to be take care. The successful working of the institution depends on a suitable timetable. Time table is the detailed plan showing the schedule of time allotment to various scholastic and co-scholastic activities. Usually timetable is prepared for a week, to be repeated. All the work is carried out systematically in tune with the timetable. Time table inculcates habit of orderliness, steadiness, regularity and alertness among the teachers and pupils. Time table helps to maintain discipline and order.

Conclusion

Institutional planning in Indian higher education is an extremely important activity as it forms the basis of all programmes of quantitative and qualitative improvement in education. Planning is the process of preparing a set of discussions for action in future directed at achieving goals. Without planning, an individual or a society, an institute or a nation cannot prosper. It was the farsightedness of Pundit Jawaharlal Nehru that he planned five year plans for the development of India after independence. Similarly any educational institution, cannot achieve the targeted goals unless it goes for proper planning. Educational planning implies taking of decisions for future actions with a view to achieving predetermined objectives through the optimum use of scarce resources said J.P. Naik. Institutional planning is a part of educational planning. It is confined to a particular institution and functions keeping the goals of that particular institution. It is one of the grassroots level planning. It ensures better and more fruitful use of the resources' which the institution has or can have. It is the institution that knows best its needs and problems that have to be solved. Hence it is the institutional planning that can best plan for its welfare and development and ultimately nation building.

REFERENCES

1. Garg, M. (2013). Leadership in Educational Administration. *Educational Administration* (Sharma, D.P). Jammu: DDE, University of Jammu. Retrieved from www.distanceeducationju.in
2. Gbadamosi, L.A. (2005), *Basks of Educational Planning*. Ijebu-ode: Triumph Publishers.

3. http://www.slideshare.net/MadamJahan/jahan-ara-shams-stages-of-educational-planning

Introduction to Educational Management and Planning, retrieved from http://www.nti-nigeria.org/nti-pgde/PGDE-21.pdf

4. *Indian higher education losing world-class scholars to foreign universities, says President.*, retrieved fromhttp://www.indiaeducationreview.com/news/indian-higher-education-losing-world-class-scholars-foreign-universities-says-president/19147

5. Kalanilayam, S. (2009). *Institutional Planning.*, retrieved from http://sathitech.blogspot.in/2009 /04/institutional-planning.html

6. Longe, R. (1987). *Fundamentals of Educational Planning*. Ibadan: Adejare Press 05.

7. Malhotra, P. *Institutional Planning in Higher Education.*, retrieved from http://peeyushmalhotra. webs. com

8. Mathur, S.S. (1975). *Educational Administration*, Principles and Practices. Jalandhar: Krishna Brother.

9. Mishra, V. & Pundir, V. (2011). Institutional Planning : The Working Principles, *Zenith, International Journal of Multidisciplinary Research*, Vol. 1 Issue 6, October 2011, retrieved from http://www.zenithresearch. org.in/

10. Thamarasseri, Ismail. (2015). *Educational Administration & Supervision*. New Delhi: Dominant Publishers & Distributors (P) Ltd.

11 Attitude of Secondary Students and Teachers towards IT @ School

Introduction

IT @ School is a project started in Kerala state of India to enabling Information and Communication Technology (ICT) integration in teaching learning arena of school education. It is one of the milestone in the school educational history of Kerala. This project gave birth to ICT revolution in schools of Kerala. Later it spread in different dimensions. "Akshaya", is one of the Mass ICT education project is emerged as a continuum of IT @ school. The IT @ school project initially witnessed several hurdles from different corners especially from old fashioned teachers. Tremendous training programmes, Governmental and Community initiatives overcome all these challenges. Contemporary pedagogical revolutions in school education also going in consonance with ICT movement. This present study conducted in Malappuram district of Kerala which is always witnessed to become the launch pad of several Pilot projects Like District Primary Education Programme (DPEP), IT @ School and Akshaya. This chapter discuss the attitude of teachers and students towards IT @ school.

IT @ School is a project for achieving excellence and equity of educational opportunities through the use of information technology implemented in the Kerala State. "Excellence and Equity in Education - No exceptions - No excuses" this is the vision statement of the project. IT @ School is project of the Kerala state government to introduce Information Technology (IT) – enabled teaching and learning in the high schools of the state. In April 2000 the government constituted an IT task force for developing a vision for the use of IT in education. This vision has been out lined in the document "IT in Education – vision 2010". The document envisions a total transformation of the classroom at all levels, information technology acting as a powerful vehicle driving this transformation.

IT @ School details the first steps towards this vision. IT @ School provides ICT enabled education to 1.6 million students per year in the state of Kerala. It endeavours to enhance the intellectual productivity of teacher and the curricular comprehension of students. The work of the project saw 4 million students and 0.2 million teachers empowered in ICT through a network of dedicated 200 Master Trainers and 5600 IT Co-ordinators. IT @ School is the nodal agency for implementing EDUSAT network and runs an exclusive channel for education called 'ViCTERS' (Virtual Classroom Technology on Edusat for Rural Schools). The project has now associated with *Bharat Sanchar Nigam Limited* (BSNL) to provide Internet broad band connectivity to all high schools in Kerala. The success of the Project can be visualised by the conduct IT practical examination in free software for about 4 million students, first of this kind in the world with so much vast resourceful deployment of free software. The efforts of Project saw deployment of adequate IT infrastructure to all schools including computers and other accessories. Single largest simultaneous deployment of Free and *Open Source* Software (FOSS) based ICT education in the world.

This project aims to integrate information technology into the mainstream curriculum of the high schools of the state in a way that enhances the intellectual productivity of teachers, enhances students' learning and improves the management efficiency of school administrators. It is emphasized that information technology is not taught as a separate subject, but used as a tool for routine teaching and learning. It is expected that in this process, all students come out of school as comfortable users of this technology, which is permeating almost all spheres of human society. It is also expected that a large number of students will be enthused to become IT professionals and take up rigorous professional courses at higher academic levels. IT @ School has four major elements. viz.;

1. A vision of transformation that is shared by all stakeholders and implemented with full participation from the local community, teachers, parents and students.
2. Extensive digital content that meets the demand for information and resources that are beyond the scope of text books.
3. Teachers who are enthused and empowered by the technology.
4. Adequate hardware to give the teachers and students smooth access to the technology.

The project sought to integrate all the four elements in its implementation. There are a number of factors that are favourable for the project as well as many that are unfavourable. The recent modernization of the school curriculum, decentralization of the state planning process, the regular in-service training of teachers and the prospect of support from the large community of non-resident Keralaites all used for the successful implementation of the project. The poor infrastructural facilities in a large number of schools, unfamiliarity of teachers with the technology, and above all acute shortage of state funding are some of the constraints. The project has an implementation philosophy that uses the favourable factors to overcome the unfavourable. The main components of the implementation philosophy are as follows:

- Technology offers no magic solutions to academic backwardness in schools. It can only provide a tremendous support to reform efforts Technology implementation has to go hand in hand with school reform. Therefore a well-conceived School Reform project needs to be implemented along with this project in order that these efforts are not wasted. Since total school reform implies considerable up gradation of the school infrastructure to provide basic amenities, massive inputs need to go into it. It would be more realistic to approach external funding agencies for this.
- The project should be implemented in phases. The ground prepared and tested before launching the full-scale implementation. It is possible to implement the earlier phases with state and local funding. External agencies can be approached for more massive inputs in the strength of the effective implementation of the earlier phases and the mobilization of local resources that has mobilization of local resources that has already taken place. Non-resident Indians (NRI) and computer corporate foundations can be approached for donations of computers or preferably funding for buying computers.
- Very little can be achieved without the support and participation of the major stakeholders – children, parents, teachers and community leaders. Therefore enlisting of stakeholder participation would be a major component of the project.
- The teacher is the Key implementer of the project. Therefore all efforts will be put to motivate and empower the teachers to use the technology in their lesson preparation, classroom instruction and record keeping.
- The state made the major initiatives for building up stakeholder support and for teacher empowerment in the first phase of the project itself.
- While the state takes the initiative for building awareness among the stakeholders, on the potentials of Information Technology to enhance education, the initiative for implementation should come from the teachers and the local community.

- There is no one solution that suits all the schools. Therefore every school that decides that technology can enrich the teaching learning process, prepared a "Technology Plan" that takes into account the special needs and facilities of the school.
- Except in certain special localities where it is very difficult to raise local funding, a major share of funding requirements for hardware acquisition met locally with the help of PTAs and local bodies.
- Rather than depending on "donations", business models should also be considered for funding the infrastructure and hardware. The business models essentially consider generating revenue from the facilities out of regular school hours. This business can be managed either by *Panchayats* or private agencies.
- The introduction of IT keep pace with the introduction of curriculum reform in high school. The initiative for developing curriculum based content will be taken by the state. Evaluation of student performance will be based on Continuous Comprehensive Evaluation involving assessment of all facets of learning and not just rote reproduction of textual information. This will step up the demand for technology-enriched teaching and learning.

Background of the Problem

Today our education system is knowledge and examination oriented that test only the rote memory of the students. The affective domain such as attitudes is neglected in our teaching. We are giving more knowledge about man and his environment. They do not take care on technology. But the knowledge increases at a tremendous speed by the development of mass media. Along with the development of knowledge, the children should also be encouraged to develop favourable attitude towards information technology. Thus the children should also be encouraged to develop positive attitude towards Information technology which is an important part of science and technology and possess application in almost all human activities. Hence the main outcome of the introduction of Information technology is the inculcation of proper attitude towards it. Therefore the present investigation has been undertaken with a view to find out how far the attitude of Information technology education developed among secondary school students and teachers of Kerala.

Need and Significance of the Study

Although a variety of strategies are available to policy makers for technology in a democratic society, information technology education as suggested is of the most viable strategy. Education can enable individuals to make personal responsibility for improving their own status and their community and nation. So information technology is bringing some exciting innovations to education. It helps the individual to take over the most of the drudgery of schooling. Computer allocate learning resource to individuals and groups. Information technology education provide easy access to files of information for reference and guidance. Information technology education engages the students in tutorial interaction and dialogue. Information technology education provides direct interaction between student and the subject matter to be learned. At present one of the agency for information technology education is the school. Thus it can be seen that computers in education at situations, promise a much needed help, flexibility and relief to the teachers, administrators, researchers and centres of learning. Information technology education has emerged as an independent discipline, one that may be of different levels. Information technology education also incorporates the concepts of computer awareness and computer literacy. The computer should be used as a tool for teaching and learning. Thus students' and teachers' attitude towards 'IT @ School' in the secondary schools must be changed and their computer needs are to be met. Favourable situations or facilities must be provided in the school to improve the growth of attitudes among the students towards information technology. Students must be exposed to the need and application of information technology in future.

Statement of the Problem

The problem selected for this study is to identify the attitude of secondary school students towards IT @ school project. So, the study is specifically stated as *"Attitude of Secondary School Students and Teachers towards IT @ School project with special reference to Malappuram District"*.

Definition of Key Terms

- **Attitude:** An attitude is a pre-disposition to perceive, feel or behave towards specific objects or a certain people or a particular manner.
- **Secondary:** Students studying in the 8th, 9th and 10th standard.
- **IT @ School:** A project for achieving excellence and equity of educational opportunities through use of information technology, launched by Public Education Department of Government of Kerala.
- **Information Technology:** The study or use of systems (especially computers, telecommunications, etc.) for storing, retrieving and sending information.
- **Project:** Project as a problematic act carried to completion in its natural setting. (Stevenson, 1989)

Objectives of the Study

- To construct an attitude scale to measure the attitude of secondary school students towards 'IT @ school'.
- To measure the attitude of secondary school students towards 'IT @ School'.
- To measure the attitude of secondary school students towards 'IT @ school' based on sex, locality, type of school.
- To compare the attitude of male and female secondary school students towards 'IT @ school'.
- To compare the attitude of private aided and government secondary school students towards 'IT @ school'.
- To compare the attitude of rural and urban students towards 'IT @ school'.
- To construct an attitude scale to measure the attitude of secondary school Teachers towards 'IT @ school'.
- To measure the attitude of secondary school Teachers towards 'IT @ school'.
- To measure the attitude of secondary school teachers towards 'IT @ School' based on sex, type of school and locality.
- To compare the attitude of private aided and Government secondary school Teachers towards 'IT @ school'.
- To compare the attitude of male and female secondary school Teachers towards 'IT @ school'.
- To compare the attitude of urban and rural secondary school Teachers towards 'IT @ school'.

Hypotheses

- There will be significant difference between the attitude of male and female students towards 'IT @ School'.
- There is no significant difference between the attitude of Government and private aided school students towards 'IT @ school'.
- There will be significant difference between the attitude of urban and rural students towards 'IT @ school'.
- There will be significant difference between the attitude of male and female teachers towards 'IT @ school'.
- There is no significant difference between the attitude of private aided and Government secondary school teachers towards 'IT @ school'.

- There will be significant difference between the attitude of urban and rural secondary school teachers towards 'IT @ school'.

Methodology in Brief

Of the various methods such as historical, experimental, case study and survey method, the investigator decided to adopt the survey method since the problem is concerned about present status of Information Technology education. The investigator selected the normative survey method for conducting the study. In the present study the investigator intended to measure the Attitude of Secondary School Students and teachers towards IT @ School project with special reference to Malappuram District. So this study aims at measuring the attitude of Secondary School Students and teachers towards IT @ School. Here normative survey method is the best method for conducting research study. A sample of 400 students and 100 teachers was selected from different secondary schools in Malappuram district. The selection of students was based on stratified random sampling technique.

Scope and Limitations of the Study

The scope of the study is limited to 400 secondary school students and 100 secondary school teachers. Limitations apart a data based study can provide valuable and reliable information regarding the attitude of the students and teachers towards IT @ school project. The study is limited only to Malappuram District in Kerala state comprising eight secondary schools.

Major Findings of the Study

From the present study the investigator came to the following findings:

- Secondary school students have a favourable attitude towards IT @ School. This result is supported by the following values. (Arithmetic Mean [A.M.] = 224.5, Standard Deviation [S.D.] = 14.7).
- The male secondary school students have a favourable attitude towards IT @ School. This result is supported by the following values. (A.M. = 138.5, S.D. = 15.6).
- The female secondary students have a favourable attitude towards IT @ School Project. This result is supported by the following value. (A.M. = 130.5, S.D. = 14.95).
- Government secondary students have favourable attitude towards IT @ School Project. (A.M. = 134.25, S.D. = 16.65).
- Private secondary school students have a favourable attitude towards IT @ School Project. (A.M. = 134.75, S.D. = 12.54).
- Urban secondary school students have a favourable attitude towards IT @ School Project. (A.M. = 135, S.D. = 16.57).

- Rural secondary students have a favourable attitude towards IT @ School Project. (A.M. = 134, S.D. = 12.63).
- The attitude score of male secondary students are higher than that of female students. Arithmetic mean of male students is 138.5 and the standard deviation is 15.6. Arithmetic mean of female students is 130.5 and the standard deviation is 14.95. The critical ratio is 5.23. That is there is significant difference between attitude of male and female secondary students towards IT@School Project. (Critical Ratio [CR]=5.23:P<0.01)
- There is no significant difference between the attitude of government and private Aided students towards IT @ School Project. Arithmetic mean of private aided students is 134.75 and the standard deviation is 12.54. Arithmetic mean of Government student is 134.25 and the standard deviation is 16.65. Critical ratio is 0.33, which is not significant at any level. (CR=0.33: P>0.01)
- There is no significant difference between the attitude of rural and urban secondary students towards IT @ School Project. Arithmetic mean of rural student is 134 and the standard deviation is 12.63. Arithmetic mean of urban students is 135 and the standard deviation is 16.57. Critical ratio is 0.67 which is not differ significantly. (CR= 0.67: P>0 01)
- Secondary school teachers have a favourable attitude towards IT @ School. This result is supported by the following values. (A.M. = 137.9, S.D. = 12.74).
- The male secondary school teachers have a favourable attitude towards IT @ School. This result is supported by the following values. (A.M. = 139.7, S.D. = 12.52).
- The female secondary teachers have a favourable attitude towards IT @ School Project. This result is supported by the following value. (A.M. = 137.1, S.D. = 12.45).
- Government secondary teachers have favourable attitude towards IT @ School Project. (A.M. = 133.1, S.D. = 9.59).
- Private secondary school teachers have a favourable attitude towards IT @ School Project. (A.M. = 142.7, S.D. = 13.66).
- Urban secondary school teachers have a favourable attitude towards IT @ School Project. (A.M. = 141.3, S.D. = 11.9).
- Rural secondary teachers have a favourable attitude towards IT @ School Project. (A.M. = 134.9, S.D. = 12.32).
- There is no significant difference between the attitude of male and female secondary school teachers towards IT @ School. Arithmetic mean of male teachers is 139.7 and the standard

deviation is 12.52. Arithmetic mean of female teachers is 137.1 and the standard deviation is 12.45. The critical ratio is 1.04. Which is not significant at any level. (CR=1.04:P>0.01)

- The attitude score of aided school teachers are higher than that of government school teachers. Arithmetic mean of private aided teachers is 142.7 and the standard deviation is 13.66. Arithmetic mean of Government teachers is 133.1 and the standard deviation is 9.59. The Critical ratio is 4.06. That there is significant difference between the attitude of aided and government secondary teachers towards IT @ School. (CR=4.06:P<0.01)

The attitude score of urban secondary teachers are higher than that of rural secondary school teachers. Arithmetic mean of urban teachers is 141.3 and the standard deviation is 11.9. Arithmetic mean of rural teachers is 134.9 and the standard deviation is 12.32. Critical ratio is 2.64. That there is significant difference between the attitude of urban and rural secondary teachers towards IT @ School. (CR=2.64: P<0.01)

Tenability of the Hypotheses

- The first hypothesis was that there would be a significant difference between the attitude of male and female secondary school students towards IT @ school. The finding related to this hypothesis was that there existed a significant difference between the attitude of male and female students towards IT @ School. (C.R. = 5.23; p< 0.01). So the hypothesis was accepted.
- The second hypothesis was that no any significant difference between the attitude of government and private aided secondary students towards IT @ School. The finding related to this hypothesis was that there existed no significant difference between government and private students towards IT @ School. (C.R. = 0.33; p> 0.01). So the hypothesis was accepted.
- The third hypothesis was that there would be a significant difference between the attitude of rural and urban secondary students towards IT @ School. The finding related to this hypothesis was that there is no significant difference between the rural and urban students towards IT @ School. (C.R. = 0.67; p>0.01). So the hypothesis was rejected.
- The fourth hypothesis was that there would be a significant difference between the attitude of male and female secondary school teachers towards IT @ school. This hypotheses was rejected based on the finding that there is no significant difference between the attitude of male and female teachers towards IT @ School. (C.R. = 1.04; p> 0.01). So the hypothesis was rejected.

- The fifth hypothesis was that no any significant difference between the attitude of government and private aided secondary teachers towards IT @ School. The finding related to this hypothesis was that there is significant difference between the attitude of government and private aided teachers towards IT @ School. (C.R. = 4.06; p< 0.01). So the hypothesis was rejected.
- The sixth hypothesis was that there will be a significant difference between the attitude of rural and urban secondary teachers towards IT @ School. The finding related to this hypothesis was that there is a significant difference between the rural and urban teachers attitude towards IT @ School. (C.R. = 2.64; p<0.01). So the hypothesis was accepted.

Educational Implications of the Study

Information Technology is an inherent part of our life today. And all over the world, they are making their presence felt in every sphere of our day to day life. From launching satellites to shopping for books, from teaching to playing games. We are at the beginning of the age of information technology which are likely to have a bigger effect on the development of human society than any of the other products of the scientific revolution. Not only has the computer made possible calculation hitherto far beyond human capacity, but it is certain to alter radically the whole of our thinking about quantitative methods in calculation. The computer is certainly no substitute for mathematical thought at least not yet. But it could stimulate mathematical thought in new directions. Several modes of approach which were simply not formerly considered because the calculations involved would have been prohibitively time consuming, are now very much within the ken of ordinary researchers, thanks to the modern high speed computers. In the modern world application of computer and information technology is receiving a high sense of special effects. For the development of information technology computers are widely used in every part of the world. Information technology is a vast developing field in industry, communication and transfer of information. The world is coming closer and closer through the development of information technology. The importance of computer application is highly increasing in the field of medicine, agriculture etc. Hence the chances for increasing job opportunities in various fields are widely opening. The findings that are emerged from the present study are summarised below:

- Male, female, government, private, urban, rural secondary school students have favourable attitude towards IT @ School project. Male students have more favourable attitude than female students. There is no significant difference between the attitude of private and government students. There is no significant difference between the attitude of urban students and rural students.

- Male, female, government, private, urban, rural secondary school teachers have favourable attitude towards IT @ School project. There is no significant difference between the attitude of Male and female teachers. Aided School teachers have more favourable attitude than government school teachers. Urban school teachers have more favourable attitude than rural teachers.
- Based on the above study conducted among students and teachers belonging to the secondary schools we can conclude that they have a favourable attitude towards IT @ School.
- Due importance has not been given to Information Technology education in our schools. Most of our schools do not have the necessary infrastructure for providing computer training to the students. Lack of trained professionals and incentives is one of the major problems. Financial commitments and lack of proper awareness and motivation also contribute to this set back in computer education.

Suggestions for Further Research

In order to make the present study more meaningful and effective, similar studies in this field could be carried out. The areas of further research indicated by the study are following.

- The present study is done only to the secondary school students. Similar study can be conducted to Higher or primary students.
- A similar study can be conducted to know about parents attitude towards ICT enabled education.
- A comparative study of attitude towards ICT enabled education may be conducted among different Districts of Kerala state.
- The study conducted is based only on sex, locality, type of school etc. Similar studies can be conducted by taking other variables like socio-economic status, age, caste, high and low achievers etc.
- The study can be extended to larger sample covering the whole state.

Conclusion

Information and communication technologies are a major factor in shaping the new global economy and producing rapid changes in society. Within the past decade, the new ICT tools have fundamentally changed the way people live. The present age is the age of technology, whereby technology plays a key role in daily lives; this also includes the education system. There are endless possibilities with the integration of ICT in the education system. The use of ICT in education not only improves classroom teaching learning process, but also provides the facility of Open and Distance learning. ICT has enhanced both formal and non-formal systems of learning. E-learning has rendered convenience of online learning to thousands of learners who cannot avail the benefits of higher education due to several constraints, such as, time, cost, geographical location, age, etc. The teaching community is able to reach remote areas and learners are able to access qualitative learning environment from anywhere and at any time. It is important that teachers or trainers should be made to adopt technology in their teaching styles to provide pedagogical gains to the learners.

REFERENCES

1. *Akshaya Profile.,* retrieved from http://www.akshaya.kerala.gov.in/index.php/akshaya-profile on 10th June 2014.
2. Best, J.W., and Kahn, J.V. (1986). *Research in Education*. New Delhi: Prentice-Hall of India Pvt. Ltd.
3. Chan, J.C. (1993). As the Computer was Turned on: A Case Study of Computer Mediated Educational Experience in an ESL Classroom. *Dissertation Abstract International*. 53(8), 10-15.
4. Das, R.C. (1993). *Educational Technology*. New Delhi: Sterling Publishers Pvt. Ltd.
5. Garrett, H.E. (1960). *Statistics in Psychology and Education*. Bombay: Vakils, Feffer and Simons, Pvt. Ltd.
6. German, Kenneth, E. (1988). *"Attitudes toward Computer Instruction"*. ERIC Data Base, Record 5 of 5.
7. Goel, D.R. (1992). Development of Computer based Evaluation Software on Educational Technology M.Ed. *Journal of Indian Education*. 16(6), 140-148.
8. Guptha, A.K. (1985). The Role of Computers. *Journal of Indian Education*. 10(5), 44-48.
9. http://www.itmission.kerala.gov.in/index.php
10. *it@school project.,* Written by Administrator on Friday, 16 April 2010 12: 44 retrieved from http://www.education.kerala.gov.in on 10th June 2014.
11. Khasuwneh & Abdqllah, A. (1989). Assessment of the Current Status of Computer Education in Jordan's Secondary Schools. *Dissertation Abstract International*. 50(6), 112-117.
12. Koul, L. (1993). *Methodology of Educational Research*. New Delhi: Vikas Publishing House, Pvt. Ltd.
13. Lioce, H.H. (1994). *Attitude towards Computers of ROC Public Middle School Teachers*. ERIC Data Base, Record 7 of 18.
14. Malik, A.K. (1992). Managing Computerisation: A Study of an Educational Institution. *Indian Educational Review*. 27(3), 1-8.
15. Odenthal, J.M. (1993). The Effect of a Computer-based Writing Program on the Attitudes and Performances of Students Acquiring English as a Second Language. *Dissertation Abstract International*. 53(8), 32-35.
16. Raghavan, M (2001) *"Attitude of Higher Secondary Students towards Computer Education"*. Unpublished M.Ed. Theses, Mahatma Gandhi University, Kottayam.
17. Sampath, K. (1984). *Introduction to Educational Technology*. New Delhi: Sterling Publishers Pvt. Ltd.

18. Shah, B., and Aggarwal, R. (1994). Teachers Attitude Towards Computer Assisted Instruction and Computer Education in Relation to Sex-Organisation and Experiences. *Journal of Indian Education*. 20(3), 7-11.

19. Tolman, M.N. (1991). *"Computer and Education"*. ERIC Data Base, Record 9 of 18.

20. Waugh, M.L. & Currier, D. (1986). *"Attitude of Computer-Based Education"*. ERIC Data Base, Record 1 of 7.

21. Webster, L. (1985). *"Attitude of Parents toward Computer Education"*. ERIC Data Base, Record 6 of 18.

12 Education for Sustainable Development

Introduction

The role of *Education for Sustainable Development* (ESD) is to help people develop the attitudes, skills, and knowledge to make informed decisions for the benefit of themselves and others, now and for the future, and to act upon those decisions. ESD is an approach to teaching and learning based on the *ideals and principles that underlie sustainability* – human rights, poverty reduction, sustainable livelihoods, peace, environmental protection, democracy, health, biological and landscape diversity, climate change, gender equality, and protection of indigenous cultures. Implementing education for sustainable development is *a long-term process that calls upon all stakeholders*, including governments, educational institutions, business and industry, communities, civil society, and individuals to play a role and to embrace the ideas of sustainable development. The word "Development" is highly misunderstood in our society. Those who are arguing in favour of environmental protection generally considering are against development. The concept of sustainable development is not a simple one, and there is no road map to prescribe how we should proceed. Yet time is short, and we are called upon to act without delay. We must move ahead now, in a spirit of exploration and experimentation and with the broadest possible range of partners, so as to contribute through education to correcting trends that place in jeopardy our common future.

Education, including formal education, public awareness and training should be recognized as a process by which human beings and societies can reach their fullest potential. Education is critical for promoting sustainable development and improving the capacity of the people to address environment and development issues. While basic education provides the underpinning for any environmental and development education, the latter needs to be incorporated as an essential part of learning. Both formal and non-formal education are indispensable to changing people's attitudes so that they have the capacity to assess and address their sustainable development concerns. It is also critical for achieving environmental and ethical awareness, values and attitudes, skills and behaviours consistent with sustainable development and for effective public participation in decision-making. To be effective, environment and development education should deal with the dynamics of both the physical/ biological and socio-economic environment and development, should be integrated into all disciplines, and should employ formal and non-formal methods and effective means of communication.

The brief definition of sustainable development as the "ability to make development sustainable-to ensure that it meets the needs of the present without compromising the ability of future generations to meet their own needs" is surely the standard definition when judged by its widespread use and frequency of citation. The use of this definition has led many to see sustainable development as having a major focus on indicators, values, and practice follows. Taken together, these help explain what is meant by sustainable development intergenerational equity. Although the brief definition does not explicitly mention the environment or development, the subsequent paragraphs, while rarely quoted, are clear. On development, the report states that human needs are basic and essential; that economic growth - but also equity to share resources with the poor - is required to sustain them; and that equity is encouraged by effective citizen participation. The concept of sustainable development does imply limits - not absolute limits but limitations imposed by the present state of technology and social organization on environmental resources and by the ability of the biosphere to absorb the effects of human activities.

In fact, sustainable development draws much of its resonance, power, and creativity from its very ambiguity. The concrete challenges of sustainable development are at least as heterogeneous and complex as the diversity of human societies and natural ecosystems around the world. As a concept, its malleability allows it to remain an open, dynamic, and evolving idea that can be adapted to fit these very different situations and contexts across space and time. Likewise, its openness to interpretation enables participants at multiple levels, from local to global, within and across activity sectors, and in institutions of governance, business, and civil society to redefine and reinterpret its meaning to fit their own situation. Thus, the concept of sustainability has been adapted to address very different challenges, ranging from the planning of sustainable cities to sustainable livelihoods, sustainable agriculture to sustainable fishing, and the efforts to develop common corporate standards in the UN Global Compact and in the World Business Council for Sustainable Development.

Importantly, however, these underlying principles are not fixed and immutable but the evolving product of a global dialogue, now several decades old, about what sustainability should mean. The original emphasis on economic development and environmental protection has been broadened and deepened to include alternative notions of development (human and social) and alternative views of nature (anthropocentric versus eco-centric). Thus, the concept maintains a creative tension between a few core principles and openness to reinterpretation and adaptation to different social and ecological contexts. Sustainable development thus requires the participation of diverse stakeholders and perspectives, with the ideal of reconciling different and sometimes opposing values and goals toward a new synthesis and subsequent coordination of mutual action to achieve multiple values simultaneously and even synergistically. As real-world experience has shown, however, achieving agreement on sustainability values, goals, and actions is often difficult and painful work, as different stakeholder values are forced to the surface, compared and contrasted, criticized and debated. Sometimes individual stakeholders find the process too difficult or too threatening to their own values and either reject the process entirely to pursue their own narrow goals or critique it ideologically, without engaging in the hard work of negotiation and compromise. Critique is nonetheless a vital part of the conscious evolution of sustainable development - a concept that, in the end, represents diverse local to global efforts to imagine and enact a positive vision of a world in which basic human needs are met without destroying or irrevocably degrading the natural systems on which we all depend.

Eco-Friendly Technology

Eco-friendly technology is the method or application used to produce a safer and unpolluted environment due to exposure of chemicals, acids used in the process of development.

It also means "being friendly to the environment". For example, you can be environmentally friendly by recycling, or by being "green", as people call it. There are also many organisations that associate themselves with the term, such as Greenpeace.

In pest control, integrated pest management is regarded as more environmentally friendly than traditional pesticide use, as its goal is to reduce pesticide use to a minimum by using a variety of less impact means, with pesticides only as the last resort. More recently, the development of biological pest control methods are an effort to go a further step to being environmentally friendly. In waste management, recycling and composting are viewed as more environmentally friendly than traditional bury or burn practices. Some cities are at the forefront of such environmentally friendly practices. Eco-technology is an applied science that seeks to fulfil human needs while causing minimal ecological disruption, by harnessing and manipulating natural forces to leverage their beneficial effects. Eco technology integrates two fields of study: the 'ecology of techniques' and the 'techniques of ecology', requiring an understanding of the structures and processes of ecosystems and societies. All sustainable engineering that can reduce damage to ecosystems, adopt ecology as a fundamental basis, and ensure conservation of biodiversity and sustainable development may be considered as forms of eco-technology.

Protected Areas and Wildlife

Forests provide a host of services in addition to revenue. The various kind of services provided by the forests are wildlife, eco-tourism and climate mitigation. Wildlife parameters are covered under national parks, zoos and wildlife sanctuaries. The statistics pertaining to the development of the protected areas and wildlife, including funds provided to various schemes form a part of this section. For management and protection of wildlife and their habitat, protected area (PA) network consisting of National Parks (NP) and Wildlife (WL) Sanctuaries has been created in India covering the forests with relatively large populations of the target species and associated ecological components. For managing the PAs, Management Plans are to be prepared which identifies conservation objectives and prescribes management interventions to be undertaken during the plan period. The All India Tiger estimation exercise is one of the most crucial components of National Tiger conservation efforts. Though monitoring of tigers population in India is being done since many decades but since 2006, the exercise is undertaken with more scientific and statistically robust approach, every four years.

Biosphere Reserves in India have been created as a consequence of Man and Biosphere (MAB) Programme of UNESCO. They represent unique communities of biodiversity or areas with unusual natural features of exceptional interest with natural and cultural landscapes wherein people are an integral component of the system. In India, the national Biosphere Reserve Programme was initiated in 1986 to serve as wider base for conservation of entire range of living resources and their ecological foundations in addition to already established Protected Area (PA) network system. They are also the protected areas extended over large areas.

Apart from the protected areas system mandated under the Wildlife Protection Act (WPA) 1972, certain areas have also been declared as biosphere reserves by the Government of India. The purpose of the formation of the biosphere reserve is to conserve in situ all forms of life, along with its support system, in its totality, so that it could serve as a referral system for monitoring and evaluating changes in natural ecosystems. The section also gives state wise statistics of Wildlife Sanctuaries, National

Parks and Zoos. In all India have 512 Wildlife Sanctuaries 93 National Parks and 63 Zoos. All national park lands then encompassed a total 39,919 km^2 (15,413 sq mi) km^2, comprising 1.21% of India's total surface area.

Natural Resources and Education for Sustainable Development

People depend on natural resources for their survival. The Earth's ecological cycle cleans the air we breathe, recycles and purifies the water we drink, provides us with food and fuel. The diversity of natural resource also provides enormous economic and community benefits through the use of biological resources in forestry, farming, fishing, recreation and other activities. However, the dimensions of our current resource use are to have access to their fair share of scarce resources are endangered. Thus, sustainable development that dimension of natural resource is important. Sustainable Development is "ability to make development sustainable – to ensure that it meets the needs of the present without compromising the ability of future generations to meet their own needs". One of the most effective ways of ensuring we appreciate the importance of sustainable development is through the environmental education process.

Human wealth is based on the use and consumption of natural resources, including materials, energy and land. Continued increase in resource use and the related environmental impacts can have a multitude of negative effects leading to ecological crises and security threats. The sustainable use and management of natural resources have therefore come into focus and have been the subject of many policy discussions over more than a decade, beginning with the summit in Rio de Janeiro in 1992 (EEA, 2005). Sustainability concept is recognized and widely accepted by scientist in this summit. As a result, governmental agencies and other stakeholders have increasingly involved science when dealing with the trade-offs associated with the maintenance environmental values involved in the management of natural resources.

Natural Resources and its Importance in Sustainable Development

Human activities are having an increasing impact on the integrity of ecosystems that provide essential resources and services for human well-being and economic activities. Managing the natural resources base in a sustainable and integrated manner is essential for sustainable development. In this regard, to reverse the current trend in natural resource degradation as soon as possible, it is necessary to implement strategies which should include targets adopted at the national and, where appropriate, regional levels to protect ecosystems and to achieve integrated management of land, water and living resources, while strengthening regional, national and local capacities. This would include actions at all levels as set out below (UN, 2002).

Drawing down today's natural resource base does not necessarily mean that tomorrow's natural resource base will be put in jeopardy (Taylor, 2002). This problem to try to understand need to examine our common future (WCED, 1987). According to the Brundtland Report, the problems facing the planet are two-fold. Environmental dimension of this problem: failure to manage the natural resource, resulting in desertification, deforestation, acid rain, global warming, ozone depletion and pollution. This report says:

> "But the results of the present profligacy are rapidly closing the options for future generations. Most of today's decision makers will be dead before the planet feels; the heavier effects of acid precipitation, global warming, ozone depletion, or widespread desertification and species loss.

This established the idea of global sustainable development through its focus on the integration of thinking about the environment. According to it sustainable development can be defined as a development path along which the maximisation of human well-being for today's generations does not lead to declines in future well-being. Attaining this path requires eliminating those negative externalities that are responsible for natural resource depletion and environmental degradation. It also requires securing those public goods that are essential for economic development to last, such as those provided by well-functioning ecosystems, a healthy environment and a cohesive society. Sustainable development also stresses the importance of retaining the flexibility to respond to future shocks, even when their probability, and the size and location of their effects, cannot be assessed with certainty (OECD, 2001).

One of the important developments, which support environmental dimensions of sustainable development vision, has come into effect with the 1992 Rio Earth Summit. At this summit conclusions regarding sustainable development were declared in a declaration called "Agenda 21". In spite of not being legally bounding, with this declaration the countries' political responsibilities about the environment are defined. In agenda 21, some basic principles about the sustainable development, which focus on the natural resource and environmental dimensions are:

- Humankind is at the centre of the sustainable development. S/he has the right to have a healthy and efficient life in accordance with nature.
- On condition that they are not disturbing other countries' environment, all countries have the right to use their natural resources according to their own politics.
- A development right which meets the current and forthcoming generations' is necessary so that environment and development should be acknowledged.

- Environmental protection should be seen as a complementary part of development process.
- In terms of ecosystem protection and development, countries shall cooperate in global association spirit. In environmental protection countries have common but different levels of responsibility.
- National authorities, in terms of "the one who pollutes pays it" principle, should make the environmental costs international and the use of economic devices improved
- As to activities which have effects beyond borders, the activist country should inform the related countries in time and provide them with necessary information.

It is important to emphasise the Johannesburg Earth Summit because it is discussed solution to environmental problems in terms of sustainable development. It will aim to contribute to the development and implementation of new and innovative environmental management policies and approaches to provide a platform for discussing and presenting new methods, tools and technologies. The biggest shift that occurred was the explicit acknowledgement of social development (in addition to economic development and environmental protection) as a core component in the Johannesburg Declaration's definition of sustainable development. Although the Rio Declaration (and other agreements since then) certainly referenced poverty eradication and other aspects of social development, it primarily emphasized the need to balance environment and development (Osofsky, 2003).

Education for Sustainable Development

Chapter 36 of the Agenda 21 of 1992 Rio Earth Summit identified four major thrusts to begin the work of Education for Sustainable Development:

1. improve basic education;
2. reorient existing education to address sustainable development;
3. develop public understanding, awareness; and
4. training. It is look at each of the four components; (McKeown, 2002).

UN Decade of Education for Sustainable Development (2005-2014)

In December 2002, the United Nations General Assembly adopted resolution 57/254 to put in place a United Nations Decade of Education for Sustainable Development (DESD), spanning the years 2005 to 2014. UNESCO was designated as the lead agency for the Decade. The overall goal of the Decade of Education for Sustainable Development is the integration of the principles, values, and practices of sustainable development into all aspects of education and learning. The Decade's four key objectives are:

- facilitating networking and collaboration among stakeholders in ESD;
- fostering greater quality of teaching and learning in ESD;
- supporting countries in achieving their millennium development goals through ESD efforts; and
- providing countries with new opportunities and tools to incorporate ESD in education reform efforts.

UNESCO's major areas of activity in the Decade reflect its core responsibilities.

- **Education** is a human right and the primary agent of transformation towards sustainable development by increasing people's capacities to transform their visions for society into reality. To implement education for sustainable development, UNESCO seeks to promote and improve basic education, reorient existing education programmes at all levels to address sustainable development, develop public awareness and understanding of sustainability, and provide training.
- **Natural and social sciences** promote multidisciplinary and interdisciplinary approaches to the wise use of natural resources and to the improved understanding of human-environment relationships, as well as promoting principles, policies, and ethical norms to guide scientific and technological development that is sustainable.
- **Culture** is concerned with the identities and values that shape the way people live, their responsiveness to educational programmes, and the degree to which they feel involved in preserving for the future. UNESCO encourages an approach to sustainable development in which people are addressed with a discourse linked to their immediate concerns.
- **Communication** is virtually instantaneous, serving as a powerful driver of social transformation. In this context, UNESCO acts as a broker for effective sustainable development by encouraging the sharing of knowledge, information, expertise and best practices, producing and disseminating scientific knowledge, and sensitizing the media to sustainable development issues.

Implementation of the UN Decade of Education for Sustainable Development

As a result of a broad consultancy, UNESCO developed an International Implementation Scheme focused on how DESD goals can be reached, using seven building blocks:

1. advocacy and vision-building;
2. consultation and ownership;
3. partnership and networks;
4. capacity-building and training;
5. research and innovation;
6. information and communication technologies;
7. monitoring and evaluation.

All Member States of UNESCO are encouraged to involve as many stakeholders as possible in activities to develop and implement policies, strategies, and activities throughout the Decade. A number of key action themes have been developed to highlight possible areas of focus and project implementation:

- gender equality;
- health promotion;
- environment;
- rural development;
- cultural diversity;
- peace and human security;
- sustainable urbanization;
- sustainable consumption.

The UNESCO World Conference on Education for Sustainable Development - Moving into the Second Half of the UN Decade is scheduled for Bonn, Germany from March 31 to April 2, 2009. The Conference is examined the relevance of ESD in improving all levels of education and its role in achieving Education for All and the Millennium Development Goals. and it act as a forum for sharing experiences and best practices, bringing together close to 700 participants representing UNESCO Member States, UN agencies, civil society organizations, youth, and the private sector.

Environmental Education v/s Education for Sustainable Development

Education for Sustainable Development has its own set of goals, a shared objective between Environmental Education and Education for Sustainable Development is to motivate behaviour change toward more environmentally friendly lifestyles (Darner, 2009). Environmental Education for Sustainable Development teaches individuals how to make decisions that consider the long-term future of ecology and use of natural resource. Environmental education "is a well-established discipline, which focuses on humankind's relationship with the natural environment and on ways to conserve and preserve it and properly steward its resources." Education for sustainable development, on the other hand, "encompasses environmental education but sets it in the broader context of socio-cultural factors and the socio-political issues of equity, poverty, democracy and quality of life." (Venkataraman, 2009). Environmental education for sustainable development needs some major objectives viz., Developing full awareness and stimulating public interest in mutually related economic, social, political and ecological issues, Enabling each human being to acquire knowledge and skills necessary to improve the state of the environment, Creating novel behavioural patterns as well as shaping individual, group, and social attitudes, values and beliefs which carry concerns for the quality of the environment. (Ministry of the Environment Bureau of Education and Public Relations, 2001)

Conclusion

The environmental dimension of the sustainable development is necessary for the continuation of the living life on the earth. Therefore, all countries in the World should follow a particular environmental policy. However, in this matter people should also be informed. Peoples' fulfilling of their responsibilities leads to a good deal of development by which the natural life is affected positively like decreasing of energy consumption and preventing environmental pollution. The thing, which is necessary for peoples' awareness is, to provide them as citizens who are environmentally aware, active and participant about environment beginning from primary school. The problem with strong sustainability is the implicit suggestion that today's natural resource base will necessarily be of significant interest to future generations. On the contrary, conserving today's natural resource base does not ensure that tomorrow's natural resource base is secure. Moving towards the goal of sustainability requires fundamental changes in human attitudes and behaviour. Progress in this direction is thus critically dependent on education and public awareness.

REFERENCES

1. Allied Signal Corporation. (1989). *Remarks*. International CFC and Halon Alternatives Conference. Washington, DC.
2. Andelin & John, (1988). *Analysis of the Montreal Protocol*. U.S. Congress, Office of Technology Assessment, Jan. 13, 1988.
3. European Environment Agency (EEA). (2005), *Sustainable use and Management of Natural Resources*, EEA Report, No. 9, 4-65, EEA, Copenhagen.
4. Keown, R. (2002). *Education for Sustainable Development.*, Toolkit, Ph.D. Thesis, Portland: Portland State University.
5. Ministry of the Environment, Bureau of Education and Public Relations. (2001). *Through Education to Sustainable Development*. Poland: National Environmental Education Strategy.
6. Morrisette, P.M. (1995). The Evolution of Policy Responses to Stratospheric Ozone Depletion. *Natural Resources Journal*, Vol. 29, 1995.

7. Organisation for Economic Co-operation and Development (OECD). (2001). Sustainable Development: Critical Issues., *Policy Brief*, 1-8.
8. Osofsky, H.M. (2003). Defining Sustainable Development After Earth Summit 2002, *Loyola of Los Angeles International and Comparative Law Review*, 26, 111-125.
9. Taylor, J. (2002). Sustainable Development A Dubious Solution in Search of a Problem, *Policy Analysis*, No: 449, 1-49.
10. Thamarasseri, Ismail. & Parey, M.A. (2014). *Environmental Education for Sustainable Development*. New Delhi: APH Publishing Corp.
11. Ugurlu, N.B. & Aladag., *Natural Resources and Education for Sustainable Development.*, retrieved from http://www.herodot.net/conferences/ayvalik /papers/environ-04.pdf
12. UNESCO., *Educating for a Sustainable Future - A Trans Disciplinary Vision for Concerted Action.*, retrieved on 12-11-2014 from http://www.unesco.org/ education/tlsf/mods/theme_a/popups/mod01t05s01.html
13. UNESCO., *Education for Sustainable Development*. Retrieved on 12-11-2014 from http://unesco.ca/home-accueil/esd-edd
14. Venkataraman, B. (2009), Education for Sustainable Development, *Environment*, 51(2), 8-10.

13 Vocationalization and Diversification of Education in India

Introduction

The divide between the educated and the illiterate, between the urban and the rural, the successful, and the unemployed, the organised factory worker and the landless labourer, is growing day by day. No nation can progress fast unless there is enough homogeneity and mobility across the society in terms of talent, education, and capability. Any solutions to give employment through large national development programmes are only temporary solutions and will use more labour in the unskilled category and bring relatively less returns and probably get into financial and organisational problems. The only true and lasting solution is to upgrade the quality of our vast human resource, so that they can work creatively and produce development. Education must lead to development, and not just supply the manpower needs brought out by development. It is in this context that we need to look into the Vocationalisation needs of Indian Education.

"Every handicraft has to be taught not merely mechanically as is done today, but scientifically. This is to say, the child should learn the why and wherefore of every process" – Mahatma Gandhi

Since the beginning of time occupational knowledge and manual skill gave, in one form man to man and from generation. This transmitting process, whatever its form of organization, has developed into the educational process that has now given rise to expansion and developments of what may be formed as vocational education. The term vocational education is meant to cover both unorganized and organized methods of transmitting knowledge, skills and competence. Vocational education refers to activities designed to contribute to occupational proficiency. Vocationalization of education means to provide a strong vocational bias to secondary education. Vocational courses should be introduced high schools along with general subjects. It implies that general and vocational education should be segregated, rather than two should be galvanized. Here we are not thinking of vocational training for one stream, but to increase the vocation oriented components of all education for all students. This is what Mahatma Gandhi intended in his *"Nai Talim"* system; this is what was recommended by the Kothari Commission (1966) report through "work experience" and "Socially Useful Productive Work".

Need and Ways of Vocationalisation of Education

Vocationalisation of Education is for achieving economic development of the country. Our country a land or plenty natural resources, even though, the lack of trained man power results a poor economy. Vocationalisation of Education is for making secondary education a self-sufficient course. It solves the problem of unemployment among uneducated. It will meet varying aptitudes, interests and talents of students. Well planned practical subjects only can meet the different aptitudes, interests and talents. There are several ways can be adopt to Vocationalization of Education. viz.,

- Vocational Surveys
- Establishing new schools in rural areas
- Counselling and placement
- Close connection with employment agencies
- Apprenticeship and recruitment programmes

Skills Development or Vocational Training

Both Vocational Education and Vocationalisation of all education will involve skills development. Whereas in the vocationalisation, the skills development is intended to build the capability to act in a variety of real life situations, the vocational education gives skills for a specific vocation under well-defined limitations. Without the general skills development, the specific skill cannot help him to survive in the competition that is life. Therefore vocational education can only be useful on a base of general skills development Vocationalisation of education is fundamental to all education and vocational education can only build on top of it and not substitute it. This has been the main reason for the problems we are facing not only in our new vocational education programmes but also the poor quality of our general engineering and technical education.

Vocationalisation – When?

In the secondary and higher secondary stages, we need to stress socially useful and productive work. They will now need to be given not only the skills but also the hardware required to do socially useful productive work and gain the work experience out of it. How much will it cost? Do we have the funds to make it feasible? We have enough field data and evidence to show that the investment made in the hardware for the school at this stage, is not only not out of our ranger but that this can help to provide critical services to the rural sector, through the educational system, with the community paying for them. Thus this can be a good basis for integrating education and rural development. Furthermore these skills allow for the secondary and higher secondary schools to produce assets for themselves and other schools at much lower costs. Such an environment will also encourage inventiveness among the students, which is a very substantial gain. Thus vocationalisation of education will cover all levels of education, but only secondary and higher secondary education will need to be considered for capital investment on this account. Between these, the secondary school should have only 'broad spectrum" skills training. The higher secondary stage may then give more modules for farther specialisation, if desired.

Vocational Education-Criteria

Any curriculum which embraces vocational considerations will include these elements:

- Work experience
- Industrial visits
- Careful vocational guidance before admission to and throughout the course
- Problem solving and the practical application of skills and knowledge.
- A relationship between the courses and employment opportunities, locally or nationally.

Vocational Education in India

Vocational education has diversified over the 20th century and now exists in industries such as retail, tourism, information technology, funeral services and cosmetics, as well as in the traditional crafts and cottage industries. Vocational training in India is provided on a full-time as well as part-time basis. Full-time programmes are generally offered through Industrial Training Institutes (ITI). The nodal agency for granting the recognition to the ITIs is National Council for Vocational Training (NCVT), which is under the Ministry of labour, Govt. of India. Part-time programmes are offered through state technical education boards or universities who also offer full-time courses. Vocational training has been successful in India only in industrial training institutes and that too in engineering trades. There are many private institutes in India which offer courses in vocational training and finishing, In Kerala, 389 vocational schools are there with 42 different courses like Commerce & Business, Tourism, Agriculture, Automobile, Air conditioning, Livestock management, Lab Technician and Agriculture.

Scheme of Vocationalisation of Secondary Education

The Centrally Sponsored Scheme of Vocationalisation of Secondary Education at +2/Higher Secondary level is being implemented since 1988. It provides for diversification of educational opportunities so as to enhance individual employability, reduce the mismatch between demand and supply of skilled manpower and provides an alternative for those pursuing higher education. The revised scheme is in operation since 1992-93. The Scheme provides for financial assistance to the States to set up administrative structure, area vocational surveys, preparation of curriculum, text book, work book curriculum guides, training manual, teacher training programme, strengthening technical support system for research and development, training and evaluation etc. It also provides financial assistance to NGOs and voluntary organizations towards implementation of specific innovative projects for conducting short-term courses.

The Scheme, so far, has created infrastructure of 21000 sections in 9619 schools and creating a capacity of about 10 lakh students at + 2 level. The grants released so far since the inception of the scheme is Rs. 765 crore. Based on the recommendations of various Committees/Review Groups, the existing Scheme is being revised. The corner stone of the National Vocational Education Qualification Framework (NVEQF) is the close partnership and collaboration with the industry/ potential employers at all stages starting from identification of courses, content development, training and provision of resource persons, assessment, accreditation, certification and placement.

India's Prospects of Vocationalization and Diversification of Education

In India, we believe that education is the key to the task of nation-building. It is also a well-accepted fact that providing the right knowledge and skills to the youth can ensure the overall national progress and economic growth. Combine the thought with the fact that India is a nation of young people - out of a population of above 1.1 billion, 672 million people are in the age-group 15 to 59 years - which is usually treated as the "working age population". It is also being predicted that India will see a sharp decline in the dependency ratio over the next 30 years, which will constitute a major 'demographic dividend' for India. In the year 2001, 11% of population of the country was in age group of 18-24 years which is expected to rise to 12% by the end of XI Five Year Plan.

This young population should be considered as an invaluable asset which if equipped with knowledge and skills, can contribute effectively to the development of the national as well as the global economy. The vision is to realize India's human resource potential to its fullest in the education sector, with equity and inclusion. The Report of the Education Commission

(1964-66) set a number of goals to be pursued. One of them was "to vocationalise secondary education." In the year 2007, Government of India announced that 1600 new industrial training institutes (ITIs) and polytechnics, 10,000 new vocational schools and 50,000 new Skill Development Centres would be opened to ensure that annually, over 100 lakh students get vocational training, which would be a four-fold increase. There are emerging shortages are there in the reservoir of skilled and trained manpower in a number of sectors. There is thus a need to expand the VET programmes to take advantage of the demographic dividend of the country and to fulfil the aspirations and right of the youth to gainful employment and contribute to national productivity.

System of Vocational Education and Training (VET) in India

The Technical and Vocational Education and Training system (TVET) in India develops human resource through a three-tier system:

- Graduate and post-graduate level specialists (e.g. IITs, NITs, engineering colleges) trained as engineers and technologists.
- Diploma-level graduates who are trained at Polytechnics as technicians and supervisors.
- Certificate-level for higher secondary students in the vocational stream and craft people trained in ITIs as well as through formal apprenticeships as semi-skilled and skilled workers.

There are more than 17 Ministries/Departments of Govt. of India providing or funding formal/non-formal VET programmes. The total annual training capacity of VET programmes thus offered is estimated to be about 25 lakh. However there is a lot of variation among the various programmes in terms of duration, target group, entry qualifications, testing and certification, curriculum, etc. which has resulted in problems related to recognition of qualifications, equivalence and vertical mobility.

Need for Vocationalisation of Education in India

Vocational Education and Training (VET) is an important element of the nation's education initiative. In order for Vocational Education to play its part effectively in the changing national context and for India to enjoy the fruits of the demographic dividend, there is an urgent need to redefine the critical elements of imparting vocational education and training to make them flexible, contemporary, relevant, inclusive and creative. The Government is well aware of the important role of Vocational education and has already taken a number of important initiatives in this area. In India, skill acquisition takes place through two basic structural streams – a small formal one and a large informal one. Details of major formal sources are listed in table below.

Table 13.1

Details of major formal sources of skill acquisition

Type of Source	Institute	Capacity	Quantity
Mainstream Education system	Centrally sponsored Scheme of Vocationalisation of Secondary education run by the Ministry of HRD	Enrolling less than 3% students at the Upper secondary level	9,583 schools offering about 150 educational courses of two years education
Training Institutions outside the school and university system	ITIs (Govt./Aided/Private)	Total seating capacity of 7.85 lakh	1922 Public & 3566 Private ITIs
Diploma Level	Polytechnics	1,244 Polytechnics run by MHRD with a capacity of 2.95 Lakhs	1,747 AICTE approved diploma programmes with 294370 seats

Need for Strengthening Vocational Education Programmes

The major reforms proposed for bringing about necessary 'flexibility' in the offering of vocational courses and development of 'modular competency based curricula' in collaboration with industry to suit the needs of both target groups and the employers (industry) will be useful in reducing the shortage of skilled manpower. In addition the high dropout rate of students after Class X is significant and a cause of worry, as evident from the following statistics:

Table 13.2

Number of schools and students

Number of secondary schools (Class IX- X)	1,23,265
Number of higher secondary schools (Class XI-XII)	60,383
Number of students in secondary schools	2.89 crore
Number of students in higher secondary schools	1.66 crore
Projected population of 14-16 age group	4.84 crore
Projected population of 16-18 age group	4.86 crore

Source: *Selected Educational Statistics (2008-09) – provisional data. Population projections are based on census data compiled by Registrar General of India.*

It would be beneficial if these children, as also a large number of children who have the inclination, but are compelled to join formal secondary schooling, to be channelized into vocational education. This would lead to a system of education which is more meaningful and relevant in the local context. Gradually the ambit would be expanded to address the needs and aspirations of those engaged in traditional means of livelihoods too. The contribution of such educated youth would boost the state of the Indian economy through the thrust of the Government on universalization of secondary education, skill development and social justice through inclusive education and training.

Conclusion

The rapid transformation of societies in their social, political, economic, technological, and education spheres has changed perspectives on the need for and nature of vocational skills. A historical change of views on vocationalization from more educational to more functional has broadened the nature of vocationalization and included separate technical courses under its umbrella. This pattern is due to the gradual blending of general and vocational programmes, which sometimes share up to 75 per cent of their content. Within general secondary education there is a diverse pattern of provision of TVET. This includes at least two levels, lower secondary and upper secondary, and is delivered within two modes, as embedded learning and as separate course/programmes. The degree to which vocationalization occurs and its nature depends on the level of economic development and on cultural traditions. Social, economic and technology rationales are used by governments to decide on their particular vocationalization policy. The industrial and labour market trends clearly indicate the necessity of strengthening of vocational education in India. The introduction of vocational education at schools will enable us to broaden the vocational education base at secondary level of education. A clear pathway for vocational students to enter higher education streams is the way to move forward. Through this concept note we have made an endeavour to provide some of the possible solutions to address these issues. Framing of a latest vocational qualification framework, renovation of vocational degrees and setting up of a Vocational University with polytechnics, community colleges, as affiliated colleges are some of the recommendations which require further deliberation at National and State level.

REFERENCES

1. Chandra, S.S. (2003). *Adult and Non-Formal Education*. New Delhi: Surjeet Publishers.
2. Joshi, A. (2013). *Vocationalisation of Education in India: Current Scenario, Key Challenges and New Directions*., retrieved from http://www.developmentoutlook.org/2013/01/ vocationalisation-of-education-in-india_9.html
3. Krishnan, D.K., & Thamarasseri, Ismail. (2013). *Contemporary Issues in Indian Education*. New Delhi: Kanishka Publishers.
4. Mujumdar, S. *Need for Vocationalisation of Education in India* retrieved from http://www.indiaeducationreview.com/article/need-vocationalisation-education-india
5. Rao, V.K. (1999). *Vocational Education*. New Delhi: Rajat Publishers.
6. Singh, U.K. & Sudarshan, K.N. (2004) *Vocational Education*. New Delhi: Discovery Publishing House Pvt. Ltd.

7. Thamarasseri, Ismail. (2014). *Issues and Challenges of Indian Education*. Agra: Shri Vinod Pustak Mandir.
8. Venkataiah, S. (2002). *Vocational Education*. New Delhi: Anmol Publishers (P) Ltd.
9. *Vocationalisation of Education; Why, When, and How.*, retrieved from http://www.vigyanashram.com

14 Developing Professionalism for Teacher Educators

Introduction

Teaching is a profession. Teacher's training is an important component of teacher education. Profession is a vocation founded upon specialized educational training. A professions is skill based on a theoretical knowledge. Professionalism is the expertness characteristics of a professional person. It has to do with how to handle ourselves in situations. A professional teacher desires to locate effective communicative skills to achieve preferred educational goals. Like every profession, in teacher education also teacher educators should develop professional ethics and code of ethics to correct himself and get self satisfaction by developing his conduct, behaviour and personality. Teachers and teacher educators develop professional ethics by imposing responsibility on himself by showing obligation towards students, parents, society, higher authority and profession.

"The teachers' place in society is of vital importance. He acts as the point for the transmission of intellectual tradition and technical skill from generation to generation and helps to keep the lamp of civilization burning". – Dr. S. Radha Krishnan

Teaching is an art. This art has to be learnt by undergoing a specific training. In the beginning of the present century, the general belief was that "teachers are born not made". But old belief has changed now. The whole concept about teacher and teacher education has undergone a tremendous change.

Importance and Need of Professional Education of Teachers

Professional education of teachers is essential for qualitative improvement of education. Teaching is a highly skilled job and cannot be done satisfactorily without a sound preparation for it. Teacher Education is important for achieving the desired goals of education and it raising the standards of education. One question that has perennially been asked is teaching a profession? Is it, like other professions, being considered exclusively as a means to a livelihood? A glance at the pages of history dispels this notion. It tells us that it has ever been an ideal vocation. Speaking about Vedic education, Lord William said that these places of teaching were constructed out of ordinary mind. Generally it was the teacher who made these huts at his own expense, and the teacher begged, not merely to make the hut, but even to feed his students. This shows that teaching has always been a profession which makes human beings, a profession with its own unique traditions. A profession should be necessarily equipped with the following intellectual tendencies.

- A profession should have opportunities for various kinds of specialized skills and abilities.
- A profession should also possess opportunities for regular and systematic promotion during the period of service.
- A profession should possess opportunities for the necessary special training and preparation of those engaged in it.
- A profession provides as an occupation and a permanent membership for the entire life of the participant.
- A profession generates its own standards.
- A profession generates the desire for service even more than for personal gain.
- A profession possesses strong professional organizations associated with it.

On the basis of above points we can say that education is not merely one of the professions, but the creative source or mother of all professions. Having accepted that education is a profession, it is essential to realize the programmes that are essential for making it a success. Education is a profession which, keeping itself completely away from black-marketing, corruption and other evil practices, gives rise to healthy traditions and thus helps to make concrete the dream of national development. When we accept that education is a profession, we must also accept its responsibilities and its burden. An analysis of the existing circumstances and the potential for the future makes it evident that there is a universal tendency towards changing the new power and energy of the teacher.

- People think that education and school are synonymous with each other.
- The sources of knowledge is multiplied apart from teacher
- Seeking education means becoming a victim of the fad prevailing in education.
- The greatest fear is that the public loses faith in the teacher.

Today conditions have changed. The teacher will have to win to his own cause all those who believe him to be maker of the nation. How can the teacher be the architect of his country?

For the improvement of teaching profession:

- Teachers should be given pre-service and in-service professional training and the latest knowledge.
- Teachers at all levels should be treated as equal.
- Teacher trainees should be kept in contact with actual conditions.
- All teachers should be given equal opportunities for developing and improving themselves professionally.
- Unions of teachers should be established to safeguard the interests of the teachers.
- The administration should seek the co-operation of teachers in its work.
- Educational programmes should be planned properly.

The profession of teaching should be developed as a technical profession. Teachers should get equality in such matters as perks and facilities. They should also be remembered when posts with social status and awards are being distributed. If these steps are not taken, the poor teacher, who is living in an atmosphere of distrust and neglect, will once again have to take to revolutionary means to win for himself what society owes him.

Need of Professional Teacher Education

Teacher Education consists of all formal and information activities and experiences that help to qualify a person to assume the responsibilities as member of the educational profession or to discharge his responsibilities more effectively. Professional teacher education is essential for:

- For giving knowledge of child psychology
- For making teaching on interesting process
- For giving knowledge of learning and teaching process
- Essential for planned education
- For development of different qualities of a teacher.

From Teacher-Training to Teacher Education

Teacher Education is institutionalized educational procedure which aims at the preparation of teachers. Previously, it was known as Teacher's Training Institutions/Training Colleges. But now 'Teacher Education' has been adopted in place of 'Teacher training'. W.S. Kilpatrick, the famous American educationist once remarked, "One trains circus performers and animals but one educates the teachers".

Meaning of Professional Ethics: Commitment to Teaching Profession

"They (teachers) will not look upon their work as an unpalatable means of carrying a scanty living but as an avenue through which they are rendering significant social services as well as finding some measure of self-fulfilment and self-expression". – Secondary Education Commission (1952-53)

If a teacher has not an ideal aim he had better to take to shop keeping at once, he will there doubtless find an ideal within his capacity. If a teacher takes to his work just to make his living because nothing else is available, he will lack the essential zeal required by the teaching profession. He must be a teacher first and the teacher last. The professional ethics demands that a teacher doesn't try to exploit school influence for private gains. He realizes that if he/she does it, he/she signs his moral death-warrant. The result is that no amount of pressure can wean him from the path of duty and justice. Authority cannot coerce him, nor can temptation reduce him in to any course of conduct, not conductive to the highest interests of the school. He fights all temptations to pad his purse with money to which he is not entitled. He does not indulge in tuitions. He doesn't prescribe/ recommend books/guides on some consideration.

Need and Significance of Professional Ethics for Teachers

Teachers are called the makers of man, the makers of a nation, and the real makers of history. It is therefore, essential that teachers should have professional ethics. The following points indicate the need and significance of professional ethics for teachers:

- Norms and ethics provide credibility to the teaching profession.
- They help in developing a sense of commitment among the teachers to the teaching profession.
- They serve as beacon light to the teachers in adhering to certain important ideals and values.
- They serve as warnings to teachers not to fall upon unscrupulous methods.
- They are constant remainders to teachers for discharging their responsibilities with a sense of purpose.
- Adherence to the norms enhance the prestige of teachers.

Ethical Code for Teachers

- Every teacher shall remain punctual in attendance and in respect of his class work and also for any other work connected with the duties assigned to him by the head, of the school.
- Every teacher shall abide by the rules and regulations of the school and also show due respect to the constituted authority.

No Teacher Shall:

- Knowingly or wilfully neglect his duties.
- Propagate through his teaching lessons or otherwise, communal or sectarian outlook, or incite or allow any student to indulge in communal or sectarian activity.
- Discriminate against any student on the ground of caste, creed, language, place of origin, social and cultural background or any of them.
- Indulge in, or encourage, any form of malpractice connected with examination or any other school activity.
- Make any sustained neglect in correcting class-work or home work done by students.
- While being present in the school, absent himself (except with the previous permission of the head of the school) from the class which is required to attend.
- Remain absent from the school without leave or without the previous permission of the head of the school.

Provided that where such absence without leave or without the previous permission of the head of the school is due to reasons beyond the control of the teacher, it shall not be deemed to be a breach of the code of conduct, if on return on duty, the teacher has applied for an obtained, ex post facto, the necessary sanction for the leave.

- Accept any job of a remunerative character from any source other than the school or give private tuition to any student or other person or engage him in any business.
- Engage himself as a selling agent/canvasser for any publication or trader.
- Ask for or accept any contribution, or otherwise associate himself with the raising of any funds or make any other collections, whether in cash or in kind, in pursuance of any object whatsoever, except subscription from the members of any of my association of teachers.
- Enter into any monitory transactions with any student or parent; nor shall be exploit his influence for personal ends; nor shall be conduct his personal matters in such a manner that he has to incur a debt beyond his means to repay.
- Accept or permit any member of his family or any other person acting on his behalf to accept any gift from any student, parent or any person with whom he has come into contact by virtue of his position in the school.

- Practice, or incite any student to practice casteism, communalism or untouchability.
- Cause, or incite any other person to cause, any damage to school property;
- Behave, or encourage or incite any student, teacher or other employee to behave, in a rowdy or disorderly manner in the school premises.
- Be guilty of, or encourage, violence, or any conduct which involves moral turpitude;
- Be guilty of misbehaviour or cruelty towards any parent, guardian, student, teacher or employee of the school.
- Organize or attend any meeting during the school hours except where he is required, or permitted by the head of the school to do so.

Developing Professionalism For Teacher Educators

Teacher professionalism has relevant significance in education in that it affects the role of the teacher and his or her pedagogy, which in return affects the student's ability to learn effectively. It can be defined as the ability to reach students in a meaningful way, developing innovative approaches to mandated content while motivating, engaging, and inspiring young adult minds to prepare for ever-advancing technology. However, this definition does little to exemplify precisely how a professional teacher carries himself or herself. Due to the growing autonomy being given to educators, professionalism remains one of the most influential attributes of education today. Teacher professionalism contains three essential characteristics, competence, performance and conduct, which reflect the educator's goals, abilities, and standards, and directly impact the effectiveness of teaching through the development of these qualities. To begin, the characteristic of competence is fundamental in an educator's pursuit of excellence. A discussion on competence focuses on three important ideas: preparation, knowledge of subject area, and defined pedagogy. The first, preparation, prepares the professional for the adversity of the classroom. From language and cultural barriers to socio-economic differences, all educators face deterrents in the classroom that must be broken down by individualized techniques. Thus, by bridging these barriers, the educator will be better prepared for classroom management and create an effective learning environment. Furthermore, by doing this, the professional teacher leads students by his or her example: one who is prepared for difficulties will be able to overcome them.

Along with preparation, a professional educator with a strong knowledge of his/her subject area has the opportunity to concern themselves with preparing innovative techniques to teach material rather than spending significant amounts of time studying the material. With the advantage of knowing one's curriculum material well, the educator has more confidence in their teachings, having already placed significant though on the material being taught. Thus, a professional is able to dwell on how to relate subject matter to the students and their cultures in an original method. The final portion of competence is discovering and assuming a defined pedagogy. A professional teacher who has a defined pedagogy has already journeyed through several trials to discover which pedagogical techniques are more effective. Although this may take years to fine-tune, a professional is willing to self-evaluate his or her pedagogy as s/he develops it, revise their edification when deemed necessary, and apply one's ideas to a practical situation. Furthermore, by acquiring a defined pedagogy, a professional creates more autonomy for him or herself, allowing for a partial release from the constraints constructed by the administration, school board, or parents.

Although competence is essential to teach professionalism, it is only useful if the educator is able to perform. Performance is the ability to effectively teach the concepts of a curriculum. A professional teacher educates so that students learn concepts and apply them to their lives. Furthermore, an educator that has a high standard of performance is reliable and dedicated. The final characteristic of teacher professionalism, conduct. The manner in which an educator carries himself or herself is a reflection on one's classroom, school, community, and educational system. Conduct is a representation of how well one takes care of himself or herself, from aesthetics to language and behaviour.

Importance of in-service Education

Rabindranath Tagore thinks; "A teacher can never truly teach unless he is still learning himself. A lamp can never light another lamp unless it continues to burn its own flames. The eminent teacher at Rugby, Thomas Arnold who said; "I Prefer that my students should drink from a running stream rather than a stagnant pool".

In-service Education refers to the education a teacher receives after he has entered the teaching profession and after he has had his education in a teachers' college. It includes all the programmes, educational social or others in which the teacher takes a vital part, all the extract education which he receives at different institutions by way of refresher and other professional courses, and all the travel and visits which he undertakes. The true teacher is a student to the end of his life. In-service education is not the responsibility of the teacher alone. It is a co-operative enterprise. It has to be promoted by several agencies.

Conclusion

A completed definition of teacher professionalism far exceeds the simple notion that a teacher be prepared in a certain manner. A professional is trained to handle all situations, as most episodes in the classroom require quick thinking. Also, teacher professionalism extends beyond one's ability to understand content; the educator must discover if the students are being reached in an effective way. With the role of - teacher becoming more autonomous, an educator must be competent in their studies, perform well under the eye of the administration and parents, while maintaining good conduct to facilitate quality communication. It is rightly said, "Dignity consists in being helpful and doing the right things in the right manner and at the right time. "A teacher would do well to prepare his lessons daily. Bagley has said, "However able and experienced the teacher he could do never without his preliminary preparation". Efforts should be made to ensure that all the work done is neat and clean, systematic and in time. A teacher is a member of the society. He lives and works in the society. In view of his special responsibilities and role, he is expected to rise above the average member of the society. His general attitude in the society should be enthusiasm and optimism. He should be a man of co-operative attitude, he should be sensitive to the needs of the society. He should be guided by the ideals of democracy, secularism and socialism.

REFERENCES

1. Aggarwal, J.C. (2003). *Development and Planning of Modern Education*. New Delhi: Vikas Publishing House (P) Ltd.
2. Ahuja, B.N. & Bhatia, R.L. (2004). *Modern Indian Education and its Problems*. Delhi: Surjeet Publications.
3. Bhatia, K.K. *et al*. *Modern Indian Education and its Problems*. Ludhyana: Tandon Publishers.
4. Thamarasseri, Ismail (2007) *Education in the Emerging Indian Society*. New Delhi: Kanishka Publishers, Distributors.
5. Rao, D.B. (Ed) (2003). *Teachers in a Changing World*. New Delhi: Discovery Publishing House Pvt. Ltd.
6. Singh, U.K. & Sudershan, K.N. (2003). *Teacher Education*. New Delhi: Discovery Publishing House Pvt. Ltd.

15

Teacher Education in India

Introduction

The Teacher Education Programmes aims to improve the quality of education by enhancing the competencies of teachers and the capacity of teacher education institutions. Teaching is an art. This art has to be learnt by undergoing a specific training. In the beginning of the present century, the general belief was that "teachers are born not made". But old belief has changed now. The whole concept about teacher and teacher education has undergone a tremendous change. Education is not merely one of the professions, but the creative source or mother of all professions. Having accepted that education is a profession, it is essential to realize the programmes that are essential for making it a success. The several education commissions and committees have offered numerous suggestions for making this profession attractive and interesting. This chapter discusses the contemporary developments, initiatives, reforms and advances in Teacher Education with special reference to India.

Teacher Education is important for Qualitative Improvement of Education. Teaching is a highly skilled job and cannot be done satisfactorily without a sound preparation for it. Teacher Education is Important for achieving the desired goals of education and raising the standards of education. Dr. S. Radhakrishnan has aptly remarked, "The teachers' place in society is of vital importance. He acts as the point for the transmission of intellectual tradition and technical skill from generation to generation and helps to keep the lamp of civilization burning". One question that has perennially been asked is teaching a profession? Is it, like other professions, being considered exclusively as a means to a livelihood? A glance at the pages of history dispels this notion. It tells us that it has ever been an ideal vocation. This shows that teaching has always been a profession which makes human beings, a profession with its own unique traditions.

Professional Education of Teachers

Education is a profession which, keeping itself completely away from black-marketing, corruption and other evil practices, gives rise to healthy traditions and thus helps to make concrete the dream of national development. When we accept that education is a profession, we must also accept its responsibilities and its burden. Dr. Carr's view is that an analysis of the existing circumstances and the potential for the future makes it evident that there is a universal tendency towards changing the new power and energy of the teacher; viz.,

- People think that education and school are synonymous with each other.
- Seeking education means becoming a victim of the fad prevailing in education.
- The greatest fear is that the public loses faith in the teacher.

Today conditions have changed. The teacher will have to win to his own cause all those who believe him to be maker of the nation. How can the teacher be the architect of his country? In the absence of a national educational policy, who will make the nation? The low salaries of the teacher are dispensed by the administration, the exploitation is done by the administration, the conditions of work are made in sufferable by the administration, and yet it is claimed that it is the teacher who will build the nation. For this, the reason is that the teacher's objections make no dent upon the mind of the legislators. The following suggestions are taken from the 21st conference of the universal teachers' council, for the improvement of teaching profession:

- Teachers should be given professional training and the latest knowledge.
- Teachers at all levels (Elementary, Secondary and Tertiary) should be treated as equal.
- Teacher trainees should be kept in contact with actual conditions.
- All teachers should be given equal opportunities for developing and improving themselves.
- Unions of teachers should be established to safeguard the interests of the teachers.
- The administration should seek the co-operation of teachers in its work.
- Educational programmes should be planned properly.

The profession of teaching should be developed as a technical profession. Teachers should get equality in such matters as scales of pay and facilities.

Professional Preparation of Teacher Educators

The National Curriculum Framework for Teacher Education (NCFTE - 2009) voices the need and importance of professionally trained teacher educators (TEs). The quality of teacher educators is central to the quality of teacher education and hence, professional preparation of teachers. Further, teachers are the most important factor that determines the quality of school education. Therefore, the content and pedagogical inputs provided by teacher education necessitate, teacher educators who are qualified and competent to provide these inputs. Hence, the competency, skills and professional development of teacher educators deserve to be a matter of national concern and calls for a deeper discourse.

Recent Policy Documents Impacting Teacher Education

- 2005 – NCF position paper declares current teacher education practices inadequate in preparing teachers and teacher educators. NCF states quality teacher education as the backbone of entire education system and teacher educators as responsible for change and calls for a more comprehensive look into the entire process.
- 2009 – NCTE recommended integration of study and observation of a Teacher Education Institution, as a part of M.Ed. course practicum. Observation, study, instruction and reflection conducted during internship were expected to fulfill this need. NCTE norms committee suggested inclusion of an internship in a college of education to impart teacher education specifically to the M.Ed. programme.
- 2010 – The NCTE Draft Syllabus for the M.Ed. programme suggests a theory dominated course with 1000 marks in 6 Core and 4 specialization courses, 200 marks for dissertation and viva-voce. Only 50 marks are allotted for field experiences and practicum. Constructivist and child-centered pedagogical studies, the integration of ICT, emerging assessment techniques, life and professional skill development, theory-practical interface are some of the key areas that are not included in the draft. The draft syllabus lays more emphasis on theory.

Justice Verma Committee 2012

Recommendations made by the Justice Verma Committee, propose a paradigm shift in the way pre-service teacher education is perceived in India. Having provided a detailed account of the underlying issues of the pre-service teacher education, the commission states that pre-service teacher education suffers from poor quality due to lack of prestige given to it as a professional preparation stage of teachers, due to poor quality of the entrants in the teacher training institutions, and the lack of rigorous method of preparation with a robust teacher education syllabus. The report states that teacher education is isolated from the university system, thus lacks connect with the developments taking place in the school subjects, making the teachers ill-equipped to teach the students.

Even if slowly, the decks have been cleared and the stage is set for implementation of the recommendations of the Supreme Court-appointed Justice J.S. Verma Commission for improving the teacher education system countrywide with a National Regulator of Teacher Education and National Council for Teacher Education (NCTE) preparing to regulate and supervise newly structured teacher education (training) programmes being launched next year (2015). Six study programmes devised by NCTE have been approved and will be offered by several teacher education institutes (TEIs) at the start of the academic year 2015 and by others subsequently.

The Verma Commission was appointed to investigate teacher education after the NCTE's Bhopal-based western regional committee (WRC) granted recognition to 291 Diplomas in Education (D.Ed.) institutions in Maharashtra in 2008. Public interest litigation was filed against the WRC's order before the Nagpur bench of the Bombay high court. On January 7, 2009, the high court bench quashed the WRC order on the ground that the grant of recognition to the 291 D.Ed. institutions was in breach of an HRD ministry directive requiring WRC to refer the applications of these institutions to NCTE headquarters in Delhi. The ministry's directive, issued under section 29 of the NCTE Act, was a response to the Maharashtra government's request to the Union government not to license any new B.Ed./D.Ed. institutions in the state, because supply of trained elementary teachers was already far in excess of demand.

Following the high court's order, several WRC recognized colleges filed special leave petitions in the Supreme Court in appeal against the high court order. On May 13, 2011, the Supreme Court appointed an eight-member commission under the chairmanship of former Chief Justice J.S. Verma, to examine the entire gamut of issues which have a bearing on improving the quality of teacher education as well as improving the regulatory functions of NCTE.

The Verma Committee's report titled *Vision of Quality Teacher Education in India, Quality & Regulatory Perspective* was submitted to the Union HRD ministry in August 2012. In a comprehensive report, the Verma Commission made 30 recommendations covering six areas of teacher education - quality of pre-service teacher education ("around 90 percent of pre-service TEIs are in the non-government sector"); quality of in-service teacher education; teacher performance and audit; strengthening the regulatory functions of NCTE; general recommendations and recommendations in respect of 300 institutions inspected by the commission in Maharashtra. The recommendations of this first-of-its-type commission were accepted in total by the HRD ministry and CABE (Central Advisory Board of Education). In October 2012, its implementation was made mandatory by the Supreme Court.

"The Verma Commission has prepared a comprehensive and excellent report characterized by transparency, engagement and constructivism. We are enthused by the report and will engage in handholding, orientation, processing, monitoring, accreditation and inspections of teacher education institutes under the supervision of the Supreme Court," promises Prof. Santosh Panda, Chairman, NCTE. Justice J.S. Verma passed away on April 22, 2013 after serving as a distinguished judge of the Supreme Court for almost a decade including a year as chief justice, and as chairman of the National Human Rights Commission (1999-2003). Subsequently he chaired several commissions including the committee which recommended amendment to the criminal law after the Nirbhaya Delhi gang-rape of 2012. But if implemented in letter and spirit, the recommendations of the J.S. Verma Commission to reform and regulate teacher education may prove to be his most valuable legacy.

NCTE prepared an Action Plan on 9th September 2013 for review and supervisionof the implementation of the recommendations of Justice J.S. Verma Commission (JVC) on teacher education. Review and Supervision of the implementation of JVC Recommendations as recorded in the Action Plan will be undertaken by the Sub Group on a monthly basis. Designated implementing agencies will provide information on the steps taken according to the timeframe specified on a regular basis.

Revision of the Centrally Sponsored Scheme of Teacher Education

The Department of School Education and Literacy of MHRD of Government of India has initiated the process of revision of the Teacher Education Scheme. The revised Scheme is guided by the following factors:

- To integrate teacher education with overall education development in the States;
- The need for expansion of capacity of teacher education institutions, especially in some of the deficit States of East and North-Eastern Region;
- Address the problem of large number of untrained teachers and the possibility of large number of persons being recruited (because of the Pupil Teacher Ratio (PTR) specified in the Right to Education (RTE) Act without possessing the prescribed professional qualification;
- Expanding institutional capacity to provide in-service training for secondary school teachers in light of the *Rashtriya Madhyamik Shiksha Abhiyan* (RMSA);

- Strengthening the decentralized structures of Block Resource Centres (BRC) and Cluster Resource Centres (CRC) to provide adequate institutional support for professional development of school teachers on a continuous basis;
- To link elementary teacher education with the higher education system;
- To develop and put in place a mechanism to monitor the implementation of the Scheme on various physical and financial parameters with pre-defined outcomes for improving the overall quality of various activities of the teacher education institutions.

The main components of the revised scheme are as under:

- Modification in Centre-State financial sharing pattern, from the existing 100% central assistance to sharing pattern in the ratio of 75:25 for all States/UTs (90:10 for NER States, including Sikkim)
- Continuation of support to SCERTs/SIEs (Strengthening and re-structuring of SCERTs, Training for Educational Administrators, including Head Teachers and Orientation/Induction Training to Teacher Educators)
- Continuation of support to Colleges of Teacher Education (CTE) and establishment of new CTEs
- Continuation of support to Institutes of Advanced Studies in Education (IASE) and establishment of new IASEs
- Continuation of support to and restructuring of District Institution of Education and Training (DIET)
- Establishment of Block Institutes of Teacher Education (BITEs) for augmenting Teacher Education capacity in SC/ST and minority concentration areas
- Professional Development of Teacher Educators
- Technology in Teacher Education
- Public-Private Partnership (PPP) in teacher education
- Monitoring mechanism

National Curriculum Framework on Teacher Education

The National Council of Teacher Education (NCTE) has prepared the National Curriculum Framework of Teacher Education, which was circulated in March 2009. This Framework has been prepared in the background of the NCF, 2005 and the principles laid down in the Right of Children to Free and Compulsory Education Act, 2009 which necessitated an altered framework on Teacher Education which would be consistent with the changed philosophy of school curriculum recommended in the NCF,

2005. While articulating the vision of teacher education, the Framework has some important dimensions of the new approach to teacher education, as under:

- Reflective practice to be the central aim of teacher education.
- Student-teachers should be provided opportunities for self-learning, reflection, assimilation and articulation of new ideas.
- Developing capacities for self-directed learning and ability to think, be critical and to work in groups.
- Providing opportunities to student-teachers to observe and engage with children, communicate with and relate to children.

The Framework has highlighted the focus, specific objectives, broad areas of study in terms of theoretical and practical learning, and curricular transaction and assessment strategies for the various initial teacher education programmes. The draft also outlines the basic issues that should guide formulation of all programmes of these courses. The Framework has made several recommendations on the approach and methodology of in-service teacher training programmes and has also outlined a strategy for implementation of the Framework. As a natural corollary to the NCFTE, the NCTE has also developed 'model' syllabi for various teacher education courses.

Reforms in Regulatory Framework

The National Council for Teacher Education (NCTE) was constituted under the National Council for Teacher Education Act, 1993 for achieving planning and coordinated development of teacher education in the country, for regulation and proper maintenance of norms and standards in the teacher education system. In the recent past the NCTE has undertaken various steps for systemic improvements in its functioning and in improving the teacher education system, as under:

- Based on the study of demand and supply of teachers and teacher educators of the various states, the NCTE has decided not to receive further applications for several teacher education courses in respect of 13 States. This has led to substantial rationalization in the demand-supply situation across States.
- The Regulations for grant of recognition and norms and standards for various teacher education courses were revised and notified on 31st August, 2009. The applications for grant of recognition are now processed strictly in chronological order. The new Regulations make the system more transparent, expedient and time bound, with reduction in discretionary powers of the Regional Committees.

- E-Governance system has been introduced by way of providing online facility for furnishing of applications and online payment of fees.
- The National Curriculum Framework for Teacher Education has been developed keeping in view NCF, 2005.
- Academic support is being provided through preparation of Manual for the teacher education institutions and publication and dissemination of Thematic Papers on Teacher Education.
- Various quality control mechanisms have been developed, including re-composition of the Visiting Teams, periodical monitoring of the teacher education institutions and de-recognition of institutions not conforming to the Norms and Standards prescribed by the NCTE.

Restructuring and Reorganization of Teacher Education

Following the approval of NCF in 2005, teacher education emerged as the most challenging sector for systemic reforms in education. The implementation of NCF required not only a new approach for syllabus and textbook preparation, but also for training of teachers. The importance of teacher education has also been recognized in the context of SSA which has continuously encountered the problem of a sufficient supply of trained teachers. Now that SSA is concentrating on quality, and RMSA is about to take off, the urgency of reform in teacher education has become all the more acute. No teacher can be successful today in a professional sense without being aware of this wide gamut of demands and expectations that children bring with them. On the other hand, the teacher's professional success and capacity to serve the system and its policy goals also depend on his/her awareness of challenges that India and its society are facing in the context of inequity, inequality, gender disparity and diversity. After the approval of the Right to Elementary Education, teacher education cannot escape the responsibility to equip future teachers, as well as the ones who are already in service, to accept the arduous task of running an inclusive classroom; no matter how limited the available facilities may be at present. Acceptance of an inclusive perspective (especially in the context in marginalized groups and children with disabilities) implies imagination, resourcefulness and a sense of agency to invent and utilize appropriate pedagogic material. Such qualities need to be developed in every teacher during pre-service training

Research Activities in Teacher Education

Educational research is that which develops new knowledge, which is then applied to the improvement of educational practice. Same is true for Teacher Education. The contributions of research to educational knowledge are easy to demonstrate through reviews of related literature. However, it is difficult to determine whether the accumulation of research findings has made an impact on the practice of education. Even when research knowledge attracts the attention of policy makers in education, they generally consider it just one source of information to use it in shaping a particular policy, or use it to justify a unpopular decision, or cut funds, or may dismiss the research findings which are contradictory to their beliefs. In spite of this research in education in general and teacher education in particular continues to grow and make its contributions to the body of knowledge. Teaching, like other professions, has a developing knowledge base that serves to guide practitioners. Knowledge generated by research is an important component of this knowledge. Teacher education and staff development programme might be considered to be a central avenue of knowledge dissemination on one hand, and of practicing it's use in varied contexts on the other hand. The curriculum of teacher education and the text books they use, determine what aspects of research knowledge will be brought to the attention of becoming teachers. The practicum and teacher induction programmes might serve student teachers and novices in learning how to use this knowledge base. Research findings constitute a regular feature of teacher education courses in the foundation disciplines, like psychology, and in method courses, but the translation of the findings into class-room action is usually left to the student teachers who find this an extremely difficult or even impossible task. Teacher education is an important field for research since the quality of teacher education has been regularly questioned. At the same time as teacher quality is increasing being identified as crucial to educational outcomes and pupil gains. Consequently teacher education researchers need to work together in order to:

- Share emerging research findings.
- Develop innovative research methodologies within teacher education.
- Disseminate innovative pedagogical methods within teacher education.
- Find new publishing outlets within an overcrowded academic field.
- Support colleagues in institutions with under developed research profiles.
- Develop important emerging themes to give teacher education research a distinctive positive.

Conclusion

Teachers deals with the most dynamic resource i.e. human beings. Teacher training programmes require continuous innovations to respond to changing needs. Conversations will help student teachers to reflect on shared personal concerns, to ask questions, to seek answers from others and this becomes a vehicle for articulating, examining and changing beliefs. Teacher training should not appear as apprenticeship, where only imitation of their lecturers/supervising teachers is done by student teacher rather it should be flexible, challenging and reflective. Student teacher should be given empowerment in the classroom/school so that he can actualize his responsibility in a better and competent way.

REFERENCES

1. *Action Plan for Review and Supervision of the Implementation of the Recommendations of Justice J.S. Verma Commission on Teacher Education*, retrieved from http://www.ncte-india.org/
2. Aggarwal, J.C. (2003). *Development and Planning of Modern Education*. New Delhi: Vikas Publishing House (P) Ltd.
3. Ahuja, B.N. & Bhatia, R.L. (2004). *Modern Indian Education and its Problems*. Delhi: Surjeet Publications.
4. Anupama, B "Teaching Practice for Student Teachers of B.Ed. Programme" retrieved from http://tojde.anadolu.edu
5. Bhatia, K.K. *et al. Modern Indian Education and its Problems*. Ludhyana: Tandon Publishers.
6. Borg, W.R. and Gall, M.D. (1983) *Educational Research: An Introduction*. New York, Longman Inc.
7. Confederation of Indian Industry (CII) (2013). *Towards Professional Preparation of the Teacher Educators*., retrieved from http://www.teindia.nic.in/
8. NCERT (2009). *Comprehensive Evaluation of Centrally Sponsored Scheme on Restructuring and Reorganization of Teacher Education*., retrieved from http://www.teindia.nic.in/
9. Rao, D.B. (Ed) (2003). *Teachers in a Changing World*. New Delhi: Discovery Publishing House Pvt. Ltd.
10. *Reforms in Teacher Education*, retrieved from http://www.teindia.nic.in
11. Singh, U.K. & Sudershan, K.N. (2003). *Teacher Education*. New Delhi: Discovery Publishing House Pvt. Ltd.
12. Thamarasseri, Ismail (2007). *Education in the Emerging Indian Society*. New Delhi: Kanishka Publishers, Distributors.
13. *Valuable Legacy*, retrieved from http://www.educationworldonline.net

16 Education for Secularism

Introduction

India is a diverse country with one of the oldest civilizations of the world. With its rich cultural heritage, it has traversed a long distance during the last 66 years of its independence. The uniqueness of the Indian society is 'Unity in Diversity', which is visible in its religions, languages, cultures and castes. The Education system of a country does not function in isolation from the society of which it is a part. India is a secular country as per the declaration in the Preamble to the constitution. It prohibits discrimination against members of a particular religion. The Indian secularism is different from the literal notion of secularism. It implies equality of all religions. India therefore does not have an official state religion. In a multi religious country like India, the spirit of secularism is to be developed in order to maintain the unity and integrity of the nation. Education should play a positive role in preparing people for a secular society. Secularism will develop in to stronger force leading to the social unity of India. Secularism is a philosophy of moral education. Secular behaviour springs in the school through various curricular activities. In India, no pure religious instruction is imparted in government or government-aided schools. However, general information about all established world religions is imparted as a part of the course in Social Studies, without giving any importance to any one religion or the others. The content presents the basic information with regards to the fundamental beliefs, social values and main practices and festivals of each established world religions. Due to this secularisation of education, tolerance in India among people of all religions is widely prevalent. This chapter discussing the educational implications of Secularism, Constitutional provisions related to secular education and the concept of religious education and education about religion with special reference to India.

The meaning of secularism different to country to country. European secularism emerge as a protest against Christianity in 19th century. The meaning of secularism different in India and Europe. Webster says, "Secularism is a system of doctrines and practices that rejects any form of religious faith and worship". Mahatma Gandhi said; "We believe in *Sarva Dharma Samabhavana* having equal regard for all faith and belief". Dr. B.R. Ambedkar explains, "Secular state doesn't mean that it shall not take in to consideration the religious sentiments of the people. All that secular state means is that this parliament (Parliament to India) shall not be competent to impose any particular religion upon the rest of the people. This is the only limitation that the constitution recognizes (*Parliamentary Debates, 1951, Vol. - III,* Part II). This term secularism incorporated in the constitution by 42nd constitutional amendment in 1976. However the constitutional frame workers have a clear cut idea regarding Secularism since constitution framing. India not following western concept of secularism fully, but indianise it. Secularism is an attitude and belief. It is not anti-religious or irreligious. It does not rejecting any religion.

The Characteristics of a Secular State/Secularism as State's Policy

- The state as such has no religion of its own.
- It does not accord preferential treatment to the followers or any faith.
- It does not discriminate against any person on account of his faith.
- All citizens are eligible to enter government service irrespective of their faith.
- Consider religion as personal issues.
- State not support any religion and not controlled by any religion.

Constitutional provisions of Secularism

- Article 25: Freedom of conscience and free profession, practice and propagation of religion. (1) Subject to public order, morality and health and to the other provisions of this Part, all persons are equally entitled to freedom of conscience and the right freely to profess, practise and propagate religion.
- Article 27: "No person may be compelled to pay any taxes, the proceeds of which are specifically appropriated in payment of expenses for the promotion or maintenance of any particular religion or religious denomination".
- Article 28: Freedom as to Attendance at Religious Instruction or Religious Worship in Certain Educational Institutions.

There are many religions in India, with very substantial numbers of followers. Though our country is itself a secular state, the constitution of our country has shown great awareness or that religious susceptibilities of the people.

- 28(1): Any educational institution drawing its total financial assistance from the governments funds must not impart education of any religion.
- 28(2): The condition is part (1) shall not applicable to any educational institutions administered by the state but in the case of an institution established by a trust or a religious body, religious education may be carried on.
- 28(3):Any educational institution which receives aid from the government funds shall not compel any individual admitted to that institution take part in any religious activities conducted in the institution or any place of worship attached to it, as long as permission to do so has not been obtained from that individual, or if he is a minor from his guardians.
- Article 29: Protection of Interests of Minorities.
- 29(1): The citizens in any part of the country having their own specific language, script and culture, will have the right to maintain these languages, scripts and cultures.

The article clearly grants to the individual the right choose his own culture and language and it also clarifies that each state and its citizen will be to choose their own language and culture.

- 29 (2): No citizen shall be denied admission in to educational institution maintained by the state or receiving aid out of state funds on grounds only of religion, race, caste, language or any of them.
- Article 30 (1) says "All minorities whether based on religion or language, shall have the right to establish and administer educational institutions of their choice".
- Article 30 (2) says "The state shall not in granting aid to educational institutions, discriminate against any educational institution of the ground that it is under the management of minority, whether based on religion or language".

The government will not impose any language of its own choice on any minority. The minority status of a group will be determined on the basis of its population. The reservation of particular groups not be considered as a violation of the constitution. No educational institution will be entitled to refuse admission to any child on the basis of religion, caste, creed or language.

Educational Implications of Secularism

In a multi religious country like India, the spirit of secularism is to be developed in order to maintain the unity and integrity of the nation. Education should play a positive role in preparing people for a secular society and a purposeful life. We hope secularism will develop in to stronger force leading to the social unity of India. When institutionalized religions gradually lose their hold on the people and the dominance of religion over other institutions is reduced, that is called secularization. According to Brubacher secularism has "no religious point of view while it has a theory of moral education". Secularism is a philosophy of moral education. Secular behaviour springs in the school from the influence of the school, through the conduct and behaviours of the teachers themselves and little in the school community as a whole. All the activities and programmes of the schools must strive for the inculcation of values of love, truth and tolerance.

The Education Commission (1964-66) on Religious Education and Education About Religion: "We suggest that a syllabus giving all chosen information about each of the major religions should be included as a part of the course in citizenship or as a part of general education to be introduced in schools and colleges up to the first degree. It should be highlight the fundamental similarities in the great religions of the world and the emphasis they place the cultivation of certain broadly comparable moral and spiritual values".

Secularism in India: India is a secular country as per the declaration in the Preamble to the Indian constitution. It prohibits discrimination against members of a particular religion, race, caste, sex or place of birth. It implies equality of all religions and religious tolerance and respect. India, therefore does not have an official state religion. Every person has the right to preach, practice and propagate any religion they choose. The government must not favour or discriminate against any religion. It must treat all religions with equal respect. All citizens, irrespective of their religious beliefs are equal in front of law. No religious instruction is imparted in Government or Government-aided educational institutions. However, general information about all established world religions is imparted as part of the course in Social Sciences, without giving any importance to any one religion or the others. The content presents the basic information with regards to the fundamental beliefs, social values and main practices and festivals of each established world religions. The Supreme Court in *S.R Bommai v. Union of India* held that secularism was an integral part of the basic structure of the constitution.

History of Secularism in India

Religions of India are known to have co-existed and evolved together for many centuries predating Republic of India. Indian civilization is among the oldest and living civilizations of the modern world. India is a country where religion is very central to the life of many people. India's age-old philosophy as expounded in Hindu scriptures called Upanishads is *Sarva Dharma Samabhava*, which means respect for all belief systems. This basic trait of *Sanatan dharma* is what keeps India together despite the fact that India has not been a mono-religious country for over two millennium. A Hindu Nationalist school of thought also proclaims that with *Sanatan Dharma* being the spirit of India, the very concept of western secularism is laid off and badly imposed. The history of Indian secularism begin with the protest movements in the 5th century BC. The three main protest movements were by the Charvakas (a secularistic and materialistic philosophical movement), Buddhism, and Jainism. All three of them rejected the authority of the Vedas and any importance of belief in a deity.

Secularism in British India

In the 18th century, when the British East India Company began to gain total control over India that ideas of secularism began to impact on the Indian mind. Until then, religion was considered to be inseparable from political and social life. The British codified laws pertaining to practices within religions on the sub-continents. This began when the Governor of Calcutta Warren Hastings set out his Judicial Plan in 1772 and 1774, this was a judicial system that codified civil, criminal and commercial laws, while family law and some property laws were still governed by Muslim and Hindu religious law, not to mention religious laws of Christians, Sikhs, Parsis and other faiths. Some see this as a part of colonial divide-and-rule policy. In doing so they laid the foundation for a non-uniform civil code which remains largely unchanged to date. This is a major complaint for Hindu politicians who insist that there should be a uniform civil code for all citizens. In India, right from the British period, main contradiction was not between religious and secular but it was between secular and communal. In the western world main struggle was between church and state and church and civil society but in India neither Hinduism nor Islam had any church-like structure and hence there never was any such struggle between secular and religious power structure. The main struggle was between secularism and communalism. The communal forces are mainly fought for their share in power though they used their respective religions for their struggle for power.

Secularism in Modern India

The Sera Monastery was granted asylum by the India and relocated to Mysore after the Chinese invasion of Tibet. After independence and partition, a large body of Muslims were left in India and hence leaders like Gandhi and Nehru preferred to keep India secular in the sense that the

Republic of India shall have no national religion and the people of India shall be free both in any individual and corporate sense to follow any religion of their choice. Thus India remained politically secular and its people continued to passionately practise their religions. It was due to Mahatma Gandhi, Nehru, Maulana Abul Kalam Azad and B.R. Ambedkar that India committed itself to secularism and its Constitution was drafted on secular lines. Secularism in India, as pointed out before, emphasised upon the principles of equal respect for all religions and cultures and non-interference of religion in the government affairs. Also, according to the Indian Constitution no discrimination shall be made on the basis of caste, creed, gender and class. Similarly all citizens of India irrespective of one's religion, caste or gender have right to vote. According to articles 14 to 21 all will enjoy same rights without any discrimination on any ground. According to Article 25 all those who reside in India are free to confess, practice and propagate religion of one's choice subject of course to social health and law and order.

Thus even conversion to any religion of one's choice is a fundamental right. In fact, in India an overwhelming majority of people are religious but are tolerant and respect other religions and are thus 'secular' in the Indian context. Even Sufis and Bhakti Saints are considered quite secular in that sense. The word secularism has had multiple interpretations, namely: an agnostic interpretation and a pluralistic interpretation. While Nehru, Mohammed Ali Jinnah, and Subhas Chandra Bose subscribed to the agnostic interpretation of Secularism, Gandhiji and others believed in pluralistic interpretation of Secularism.

The Preamble to the Constitution of India grants "liberty of thought, expression, belief, faith and worship" immediately after proclaiming that India is a "Sovereign Socialist Secular Democratic Republic." This reading of the constitution suggests that the Constitution of India has a pluralistic interpretation of Secularism. Also, religious belief governs the application of laws in India (Indian law), which indicates a pluralistic interpretation of the term Secularism in the Indian legal system. The science of the concept of legal pluralism and the study of legal pluralism as it has naturally existed in India is on-going.

There are some atheists and secularists who reject religion in its entirety but such people are extremely few. Though there are no census figures available but one can safely say that there are less than 0.1% in India. Also, there are extremely orthodox people who exhibit rigidity and intolerance towards other faiths though of course not on communal grounds but on the grounds of religious orthodoxy but they too are in very small minority. Tolerance in India among people of all religions is widely prevalent. It is perhaps due to influence of ancient Vedic doctrine that truth is one but is manifested in different forms. Thus the real spirit of secularism in India is all-inclusiveness, religious pluralism and peaceful co-existence. However, it is politics, which proved to be divisive and not religion. It is not religious leaders by and large (with few exceptions) who divide but politicians who seek to mobilise votes on grounds of divisive identities like religion, caste and ethnicity. In a multi-religious society, if politics is not based on issues but on identities, it can prove highly divisive. Politicians are tempted to appeal to such identities rather than to solve problems. The medieval society in India was thus more religiously tolerant as it was non-competitive. The modern Indian society, on the other hand, has proved to be more divisive as it is based on competition.

Conclusion

One of the most ancient civilizations of the world, India can take legitimate pride in having been a civilizational unity without a break for more than 5000 years. India's contribution in the field of art, sculpture, architecture, mathematics, science, medicine etc is well known. Some of the oldest, deepest and most sublime philosophical thought and literature was born in India. India have several historical monuments or great archaeological value spread over the entire country. These include forests, palaces, temples, masjids, mandirs etc. As to this territory had the honour of being the birth place of several great religions like Hinduism, Buddhism, Jainism and Sikhism. Our past has shown us the path of peace, love, non-violence and truth. As accountable citizens, it is the responsibility of all of us to work for the preservation of this rich heritage and its cultural values and live in love and harmony. These are the foundations of our citizenship. All of us are supposed to maintain the dignity of the constitution, by not indulging in any activities in violation of the letter of spirit of the constitution. India is a vast country with many languages, sub-cultures, religions and ethnic diversities, but the essential unity of the country is epitomized in the one constitution, one flag, one people and one citizenship. We are governed and guided by this constitution irrespective of caste, religion, race, sex etc. We must put the nation above our narrow personal interests and then only we will be able to protect our hard-earned freedom and sovereignty. Education should play a positive role in preparing people for a secular society.

REFERENCES

1. Thamarasseri, Ismail. (2007). *Education in the Emerging Indian Society*. New Delhi: Kanishka Publishers.
2. http://en.wikipedia.org/wiki/Secularism_in_India
3. Kashyap, C.S. (2005). *Our Constitution- An Introduction to India's Constitution and Constitutional Law*. New Delhi: National Book Trust, India.
4. Pylee, M.V. (2005). *An Introduction to the Constitution of India*. New Delhi: Vikas Publishing House (P) Ltd.

17 Educational Initiatives in Kerala

Introduction

The Kerala State in India has a great tradition in education. It has been and continues to be a model to other states in the country. There are many factors that made these achievements possible, including the free and universal school education and the high level of awareness among the people. The global trends in education guided by the latest researches do have an impact on the education system of the state. Education scene in Kerala has witnessed many significant changes in tune with the education reforms at the national level as well as the education policies of different governments at the state level. There have been lots of debates on access, equity, and quality of education over the years and they peaked in the last two decades. Kerala has grown to become a state that gives core importance to implement latest technologies in education. Much development has been taken place in the state as a part of these educational reforms. And many discussions are done to improve the access, equity and quality of education, in the last one and a half decade. Unfortunately, these reforms have failed to achieve the comprehensive goals of education. Whether we have attained growth in the sector at par with the human resource of our state is yet to be considered. In this chapter the author trying to formulate a balance sheet of Kerala Education. This chapter tests the hypothesis that successes which have been achieved by the 'Kerala model' are mainly a result of education.

Kerala is often praised as being more developed, in some respects, than the rest of India: several development indicators, such as literacy rates and health, suggest that Kerala is much more successful than the rest of India. However, a growing minority of observers have expressed disappointment with Kerala. Kerala is poorer than we might expect given its high literacy rate; other writers argue that women in Kerala are not as empowered as previous researchers implied. This 'education hypothesis' is contrasted with various other possible explanations of Kerala's success, which suggest Kerala is unique in some way - for reason(s) which are disputed and which often seem impossible to test by scientific analysis. However, Kerala is not successful in every respect; this chapter examines some remaining problems in Kerala. Kerala stands far ahead than other states of the country in the field of education. Majority of the people are aware of education, which itself has led to many reforms in the educational sector in the last few decades to provide qualitative and effective education.

The School Education in Kerala: The School Education in Kerala has seen lots of reforms of different hues and shades over the years. The curriculum and pedagogical reforms implemented in the state have been subjected to intense debates and criticism from different quarters of the society. The theoretical and structural changes in school education brought about by contemporary programmes like District Primary Education Programme (DPEP), Sarva Siksha Abhiyan (SSA) and Rashtriya Madhyamic Shiksha Abhiyan (RMSA). The impact and influence of different syllabi on the quality of education and the social consciousness of people is noteworthy. Despite spending a lot of money on education we are yet to make consistent and lasting positive trends in our education system. Developing a system that addresses both the exceptionally talented and the students with special needs is very important. The scope and use of technology in the school education and recent trends in assessment and evaluation is also a matter of discussion. One of the aims of decentralization of school governance was increased and effective community participation. We are yet to make an honest assessment of this. There is a need for an unbiased evaluation on the effects of transferring the governance of schools to the respective local bodies. The working of the Department of Education, SCERT, DPI, Pariksha Bhavan, DDE, DEO, AEO etc. as well as the increased political interference and its negative effects on the effective governance of the school system. The new trends and ideas in school governance globally will also be a point of discussion in keeping an eye on how these will be beneficial to the school system in Kerala.

Higher Education: Over the last two decades, Higher Education has been a topic of intense debate at different levels. The emerging trends and new perspectives in higher education globally and the possibilities of these in the context of Kerala are widely discussed by different medias in several occasions. The new developments in higher education post globalization and it utilisation for the benefit of the student community of Kerala in particular is need to be discussed. The quality of higher education is a major is debate of discussion. The issues of access and equity in higher education for the different disadvantaged sections of the society, including various religious and social groups, students from remote geographical locations and girl students need to be deeply debated. The need of teacher improvement programmes and their quality, the policies pertaining to access and equity implemented in the state and the country also analysed. The academic and non-academic governance of the university is of utmost importance in higher education. The mechanisms needed for administration of the universities and their effectiveness, the undesirable political interventions and its effects on the university education are also debated. The administrative culture and activities of modern international universities and their scope and desirability in the Kerala context is interesting. Research in India is a hot subject in the academic circles. It is believed that there are not many productive research projects taking place in universities of Kerala.

Different ancient, modern and post modern Educational Philosophies, both religious and materialistic, have a place of their own in our society, and all of them have different and diverse views on education. Developing an integrated educational philosophy in our unique social setup is a very relevant topic of discussion. There are different and contradictory views on Educational Financing around the world. Resource collection from the different segments of the society and utilization of the resources in education, the fund distribution in the higher education sector, the new trends in fund raising all debated. The privatization policies that gained momentum in the early 1990s caused huge changes in the field of education in India. It led to establishment of many self-financing colleges in the Kerala state.

Alternative Educational Approaches: Outside the mainstream education system, lots of Alternative Educational Approaches have evolved and have been making their presence felt all over the world. There is an increased need for a debate on these alternative approaches to education. More often than not, these debates are centred on the *de-schooling* only. The works and contributions of different socio-religious groups in the milieu of education unique to their culture need to be discussed widely. There are deliberations on inclusive education that meets the needs of differently-abled. Technical education is an important segment in the education system of Kerala. There are many ITIs, polytechnics, technical schools, vocational higher secondary schools providing job-oriented courses across the length and breadth of the state. It is high time that we discuss the quality, curriculum, and syllabi of these programmes. Apart from discussing the comprehensive reforms and the new courses that need to be developed considering the emerging job opportunities and the particular social circumstances in Kerala.

Kerala Education – Some Flashbacks: The importance and antiquity of education in Kerala is underscored by the state's ranking as among the most literate in the country. The local dynastic precursors of modern-day

Kerala - primarily the Travancore Royal Family, the Christian missionaries, The Nair Service Society (NSS), Sree Narayana Dharma Paripalana Yogam (SNDP) and Muslim Educational Society (MES) - made significant contributions to the progress on education in Kerala. There were many *sabha mathams* that imparted Vedic knowledge. Apart from *kalaris*, which taught martial arts, there were village schools run by *Ezhuthachans* or *Asans*. Christian missionaries brought the modern school education system to Kerala.

The Kerala school of astronomy and mathematics was founded by Madhava of Sangamagrama in Kerala, which included among its members: Parameshvara, Neelakanta Somayaji, Jyeshtadeva, Achyuta Pisharati, Melpathur Narayana Bhattathiri and Achyuta Panikkar. The school flourished between the 14th and 16th centuries and the original discoveries of the school seems to have ended with Narayana Bhattathiri (1559-1632). In attempting to solve astronomical problems, the Kerala school independently created a number of important mathematics concepts. Their most important results - series expansion for trigonometric functions - were described in Sanskrit verse in a book by *Neelakanta* called *Tantrasangraha*, and again in a commentary on this work, called *Tantrasangraha-vakhya*, of unknown authorship. The theorems were stated without proof, but proofs for the series for sine, cosine, and inverse tangent were provided a century later in the work *Yuktibhâcâ* (c.1500-1610), written in Malayalam, by Jyesthadeva, and also in a commentary on *Tantrasangraha*.

Their work, completed two centuries before the invention of calculus in Europe, provided what is now considered the first example of a power series (apart from geometric series). However, they did not formulate a systematic theory of differentiation and integration, nor is there any direct evidence of their results being transmitted outside Kerala.

Missionary initiatives in Kerala: Education in Kerala had been promoted during British rule in India by Christian missionaries who were keen on providing education to all sections of society and on strengthening of women, without any kind of discrimination. The contributions of Catholic priests and nuns has been crucial and has played a major role in the education of women and members of lower strata of society, resulting in the surpassing of many social hurdles. A significant figure in the 19th century was Rev.fr. Kuriakose Elias Chavara, who started a system called "A school along with every church" to make education available for both poor and rich. That system still continues in the present. His work has resulted in the promotion of education for girls and has become a model for the educational system in Kerala after independence. Kerala's high literacy rate is attributed to a high literacy rate among girls; as it is said, "When a woman is educated, she will make sure that her children are well-educated."

Educational expansion in Kerala during the 19th century is mainly attributed to the missionary activities. Missionaries are acknowledged as the pioneers of English education in the state. Their major educational efforts and programmes not only emphasized the role of education as an instrument of enlightenment and empowerment but also showed how they were instrumental in influencing other agencies including government and other communities in establishing schools.

The history of educational efforts during the 19th century highlighted the contribution made by the Christian missionaries in Kerala. The earliest of European Christian missionaries to come for proselytization work in Kerala were the Roman Catholics. They worked mainly among the lower castes, particularly the fishermen communities of the coast. Their major concern was providing religious education for prospective priests and their educational efforts were limited to the opening of a few seminaries and some schools for the fishermen communities. The major contributions to mass literacy were made by Protestant missionaries. Since their religion was very much based on the Gospels, the spread of their religion required at least the basic faculties of reading and writing. Hence the Protestants considered educational activities a pre-requisite for their religious work. Rev. Ringletaube, the first Protestant missionary to evangelise in Travancore, started a school in the village of *Mylady* in 1806.

The missionary agencies that operated in Travancore since the beginning of the 19th century were the London Missionary Society (LMS) in the South and Church Missionary Society (CMS) in the central and northern areas. In Malabar, it was the Basel Evangelical Mission which took control of the educational efforts in the early 19th century. Although there was a heavy accent on religious subjects in missionary schools, their syllabus did not neglect secular subjects altogether. They also chose Malayalam or Tamil as the medium of instruction in these schools. Missionaries started both English and vernacular schools all over Kerala from 1806.

Education of the lower castes-both *Ezhavas* and *Shanars* as well as of slave castes was an exclusive preserve of the missionary schools till the government came into the field by the end of 19th century. As early as 1839 the missionaries are reported to have prepared a plan for the emancipation and education of the children of slaves in Cochin and Travancore. They not only started separate schools for lower caste children but also admitted them in regular school. These schools were open to all castes during a period when the government neglected the development of education for the lower castes. In the schools, children of different castes were put together under one roof, which was itself a matter amounting almost to a social revolution in those days.

Another area in which missionaries were active was that of female education. They started girl schools to surmount the reservation on the part of the parents to send their daughters to mixed schools. To promote female education, a pamphlet entitled "On the advantages of female education" was printed and distributed free by the missionaries. There were 15 girls' schools and 361 girl students in Southern region alone by 1837. The missionaries were the first to appoint female teachers for inspiring the parents to send their girls to schools, a measure which took into account the reality of the situation.

Technical training was also an area which was initiated by the missionaries. Trade schools were started with the aim of raising up a class of Christian artisans for construction of mission building. Subjects taught in these schools included printing, book-binding, tanning and currying of leather etc. Thus it was found that missionary activities were in the areas of lower caste education, female education and technical training, areas neglected by traditional system and not yet taken up by the government. However, the government supported all their activities with aids in cash and kind like thousands of acres of land, timber and other building materials and labourers. Local public also donated liberally. Missionaries also used all the influences at their command over their laity to raise monthly subscriptions from the households both in cash and kind. The contribution made by the missionaries to the cause of education during the 19th century was significant not purely in terms of the numbers that they turned out, but in terms of awareness that their efforts instilled in the minds of the depressed classes about their social rights and the minds of the higher castes in society about the danger to their social power inherent in giving a free hand to the missionaries in the field of education. The missionary activities had also an effect on the governments' educational policy. Government feared that the missionary activities might lead to large conversion. Kings and high caste Hindus were very suspicious about the missionary activities in the field of education. Hence the government started a large number of government and other private schools with a view to countering the growing influences of the missionaries and to attract large section of the people who had kept away from Missionary schools.

Thus it is seen that missionary activities both directly and indirectly made significant contributions in the field of education. They have initiated modern education in many parts of the state in the first half of the 19th century. Their involvement in the vernacular education made considerable contributions to the spread of mass literacy.

Kerala Education Today: Schools and colleges are mostly run by the government, private trusts, or individuals. Each school is affiliated with either the Indian Certificate of Secondary Education (ICSE), the Central

Board for Secondary Education (CBSE), Kerala State Education Board or the (NIOS). English is the language of instruction in most private schools, while government run schools offer English or Malayalam as the medium of instruction. Government run schools in the districts bordering Karnataka and Tamil Nadu also offer instruction in Kannada or Tamil languages. A handful of Government Sanskrit Schools provide instruction in Sanskrit supplemented by Malayalam, English, Tamil or Kannada. After 10 years of secondary schooling, students typically enrol at Higher Secondary School in one of the three streams - humanities, commerce or science. Upon completing the required coursework, students can enrol in general or professional degree programmes. Kerala topped the Education Development Index (EDI) among 21 major states in India in year 2006-2007.

Quality of Education: In spite of the large number of educational institutions in the state, the quality of education at all levels in Kerala has been showing a decline due to financial constraints resulting from quantitative expansion of the sector. A study published in 1999 by the Centre for Socio-economic & Environmental Studies states that while the dropout rates are very low in primary schools, the same increases in the ninth and the tenth standards in Kerala. This is particularly true about SC/ ST students. Schools showed that only 73% of the students joining at 1st Standard reach the 10th Standard. In the case of scheduled caste students, only 59% reach the 10th standard. 60% of Scheduled Tribe students drop out by the 10th standard. Another major indicator of the inefficiency of Kerala's school education system is the large-scale failure of the students in the matriculation examination. Only about 50% of the students who appear for the examination get through. But at present the percentage of results has been considerably increased because of major interventions by the government in the areas of curriculum and teacher training. In March 2015, 98.57% students qualified for higher studies in the matriculation Examination.

Universalisation of Education: Relative roles of the State and Private sector: Recently Kerala has witnessed the entry of a large number of self financing institutions in both school (mostly English medium) and higher education sectors. They charge high fees and are run largely on commercial lines. Fees cover not only the recurring costs, but also the capital costs. Even the government agencies are engaged in this commercial venture making access to higher and technical education dependent entirely on the paying capacity of the students. It is the government's inability and unwillingness due to financial difficulty which has led to mushrooming of self financing institutions in Kerala. It appears that the pendulum has been swinging from one extreme of near total fee subsidy to the other extreme of zero subsidy. This situation is unheard of even in the most conservative capitalist countries. At present, the government has no effective control over these institutions. The task now is to restore the lost balance between the role of the government and the private agencies in management and financing. Terms of relationship between the two have to be re-negotiated without sacrificing the larger long term societal goals.

Research in Kerala: Kerala Education system is neither research oriented nor updated. Hence research aptitude is not properly developed during the course of study. This is the one of the main reason why Kerala is not getting a broad exposure in the research field. Nowadays students are more attracted towards professional studies so as to settle with a job soon after finishing the course. This restricts the number of enrolments for Ph.D. degree in various universities in Kerala. Apart from these the deficiency and delay of fund also affects the progress of the research work. Lacks of expertise, resources, mobilization, and dissemination of research output to the society are the other major problems encountered in the research field. A careful analysis of the situation is necessary to eliminate the trend and for the building of the research sector. PhD is mostly a self driven and self taught degree with the PhD programme and the supervisor gently aiding the process. The PhD programme and supervisor should help mostly in creating a favourable atmosphere and pleasant environment in which the scholar gets motivated to excel. A committee should be formed at the university level to address the problems faced by the research scholars. Also reasonable fund shall be allotted to the scholars analysing their research needs. A general awareness has to be extended to the future generation on the possibility of research as a career since it is vital for the prosperity of any state. Even though research is tough, it is extremely rewarding and satisfying career.

Mass media and its impact on Kerala education: Kerala is one of the highly media alert society. Media playing a major role in societal development and educational enhancement. An informed society features continuous evolution and increment of quality and quantity. At its turn a progressive society can assure places of work and as a result a higher quality of life and financial stability of the population. This is the reason why we tend to a more informed society. And an informed society is built by/of/and for educated people. Passage to an informed society is a gradual and difficult process, but not an impossible one. First of all, it should be done on all levels (cultural, social, and politic). Second, it should be implemented beginning with youngest representatives of society, inserting the newest informing methods in educational institutions. Finally, and the most important, to assure free access to information and effective means.

Dozens of newspapers are published in Kerala. The principal languages of publication are Malayalam and English. The most widely circulating

Malayalam-language newspapers include Malayala Manorama, Mathrubhumi, Madhyamam, Suprabhaatham, Kerala Kaumudi, Desabhimani, Deepika, Mangalam, Janayugam, Thejas, Varthamanam, Chandrika, Janmabhumi, Siraj, Udaya Keralam and Metro Vaartha. Among list of Malayalam periodicals major Malayalam periodicals are Mathrubhumi weekly, Madhyamam weekly, India Today Malayalam, Dhanam, Chithrabhumi, Balarama, Thejas, Kanyaka and Bhashaposhini.

Internet service was started by ISPs like Kerala Telecommunication and VSNL in the year 1998. In the same year BPL, a private mobile service provider introduced mobile telephony in Kerala. Doordarshan is the state-owned television broadcaster. Multi system operators provide a mix of Malayalam, English, and international channels. The first group to enter the television field was Asianet in 1993, followed by Surya TV in 1998. Kairali TV started broadcast in the year 2000. Multiple channels then started broadcasting including general entertainment channels like Jeevan, Amrita, Jai Hind, Asianet plus, Kiran TV, Kairali We, news channels like Indiavision, Asianet News, Reporter TV, Manorama News, Kairali People, Mathrubhumi News, Media One TV and religious channels like Shalom, PowerVision TV. The only government owned channel in Malayalam is Versatile ICT Enabled Resource for Students (VICTERS) educational channel which is working under IT @ School Project of General Education department of Kerala.

In Kerala, Radio had a very vital role in communication. All India Radio, the national radio service, reaches much of Kerala via its Thiruvananthapuram 'A' Malayalam-language broadcaster. Radio Alakal, the first Community radio in the state, started narrowcasting from Trivandrum on 1 May 2006. Kerala's First private FM station, Radio Mango 91.9, was launched on 29th, November 2007 in Calicut, sparking off the FM revolution in the state. Today, Kerala has a host of private FM channels that are fast gaining influence among its population.

The history of Malayalam cinema begins with Vigathakumaran a silent film made by J.C. Daniel in 1928. The first Malayalam talkie, Balan, came out in 1938. Udaya Studio, the first professional film studio of Kerala was set up in Alappuzha by Kunchako in 1947. Another landmark was the release of Chemmeen in 1966, directed by Ramu Kariat, which won the President's Gold Medal for the best Indian film. The first co-operative society for film production, Chitralekha Film Co-operative was promoted by Chithralekha Film Society. This first film society of Kerala was started in 1964 by Adoor Gopalakrishnan and Kulathur Bhaskaran Nair.

Kerala Model of Development and Investment in Education: Kerala is the only State which follows the recommendation of Kothari Commission by spending about 6% of its SDP on Education. The Kerala model of development is characterized by high investment in Education and health that giving rise to high physical quality of life. This has led to Kerala achieving an unprecedented social development and scores high on all social indicators well ahead of all the other States in India. But the economic development does not keep pace with the social development, the indices of which is even comparable with developed countries. Kerala's achievement in education lies in high literacy rates, free and universal primary education, low dropout rates at the school level, easy access and gender equality. The growth of education has got hastened with the social reform movements but the State could not maintain the attainments made and failed to meet the challenges of rising demand for funds, enrolment expansion etc. From the fifth five year plan onwards the expenditure on education in Kerala marked a decline. And melancholy the share of education in total budgetary expenditure has been declining steadily from 32.5% during fifth plan to 27% during eighth plan. The inadequate provision for Kerala education sector by planning commission and finance commission, the reduction in funding by central govt funding agencies like UGC, declining investments by private management and local bodies, inadequate.

Through the literacy Act under taken by the Government nationwide, most of the States has achieved more than 40 percent literacy in most of the states even decades ago. And Kerala is leading much ahead of other parts of India in achieving the goal of universalizing the elementary education. The state ranked first in Human Development Index (HDI) among all other States in India. Kerala despite being honoured for its literacy level has got a struggling situation to hold back its HR due to lack of opportunities in home state. So Kerala now viewed as a state with raw materials for the socio-economic profusion but prodigality towards non-value based and non-skilled educational style of mugging up paper knowledge ruined the quality of outcomes and cease the socio-economic growth. Even by 1971, a little over 60 percent of Kerala's population was literate against the 29 percent of all India. Now Kerala becomes the supplier of brains and talents to other states and globally, not being used for self opulence.

Conclusion

The Investment in Education will be reflected in the National Income and Economic Growth of a State. At some point it is contentious to ask about the relationship between economic growth and social growth. What should come first or what leads to the other, it is almost like debating about egg & hen. The stress must be given to the factor which is essential for both, i.e. "Education" and its application. But what if the former is in abundance and later lacks. And this is not a situation that is in papers but in real world. Looking on to the scenario that was mentioned before, it can be found that it is not a suddenly occurred oddity rather it budded and grew along with the competitiveness and propensity to acquire knowledge. These are when talking in global perspective, but if considering nationally and locally it is shocking that the number of educated unemployed are growing at an alarming rate which again results to drag in economic as well as social growth.

REFERENCES

1. History of Educational initiatives in Kerala., retrieved on 03-08-2015 from http://shodhganga.inflibnet.ac.in:8080/jspui/bitstream/10603/6358/9/09_chapter%203.pdf
2. https://en.wikipedia.org/wiki/Media_in_Kerala
3. *Influence of the mass-media to educational process.*, retrieved on 05-08-2015 from http://www.educativ.info/edu/fact3e.html
4. Joachim, M.M. & Rasheed, R. (2015). Kerala Education System: De-Crowning? *Kerala Education - Issues & Challenges.*(Thamarasseri, I.) New Delhi: APH Publishing Corp.
5. Parvathy K.G. & Noujas V. (2015). Research Scenario in Kerala – An Overview. *Kerala Education - Issues & Challenges.* (Thamarasseri, I.) New Delhi: APH Publishing Corp.
6. Salim, A.A. (2015). Educational Development in Kerala: A Focus on Major Issues. *Kerala Education - Issues & Challenges.* (Thamarasseri, I.) New Delhi: APH Publishing Corp.
7. Simister, J. *Assessing the 'Kerala Model' Education is Necessary but not Sufficient.*, retrieved on 03-08-2015 from http://sad.sagepub.com/content/6/1/1.abstract
8. Thamarasseri, I. (Ed.) (2015). *Kerala Education – Issues & Challenges.* New Delhi: APH Publishing Corp.
9. The Hindu Business Line. *Quality of Education on Decline in Kerala.*, retrieved on 6 December 2014 from www.thehindubusinessline.in

18 Changing Quality Systems in Indian Higher Education

Introduction

Education is the prime mover of the society. It determines the role and approach for the modernisation of society and the nation at large. Since 'development' is the buzz word for the advancement of our nation, the quality of our education is of paramount importance along with access and equity to tap rich dividends from our demographic capital. Higher education has to be assessed from a broader perspective in the context of various types of changes in the micro and macro environment. With globalisation and liberalisation, we are players in the global arena. We need to relook at the contents of our educational system and the quality of curriculum transaction, research and development to enhance the quality of education through an effective quality management system.

Education is vital to the Human Resource Development (HRD) and empowerment in the stages of growth of a nation. Education plays a major role in imparting knowledge, values, and developing skills and, in the process, increase the growth and productivity of the country. Education in India, has reached a remarkable height, since independence. Successive governments have had to address a number of key challenges with regard to education policy throughout these days. India's huge pool of young people might be considered its biggest strength. Unfortunately, India is far from having its act together when it comes to figuring out how to educate these young people. India suffers quantity as well as a quality challenge in higher education. To be a major global player, India needs to take a hard look at its educational system and work towards quality enhancement. This chapter discussing changing quality scenario in Indian higher education, the need to reform the quality management system, functions of the universities in the changing world, and Indian universities and their tryst with global rankings.

There is tremendous quantitative expansion of higher education institutions since independence. However the quality is deteriorating. It is commonly observed that on an average, Indian colleges and universities do not perform a commendable job and are definitely not world class. An analysis of institutions reveals that only a fraction of them are accredited during a span of 20 years. There is no programme accreditation except for the technical institutions. The mind set of most of the higher education institutions is to adopt a laissez-faire approach with no aspiration or motivation to assume additional responsibilities for quality improvement. There are many quality gaps with respect to curriculum design and development, teaching, learning and evaluation, research consultancy and extension, infrastructure and learning resources, student support and progression, governance, management and leadership.

Changing Quality System and Scenario

Research and Development is the weakest link in the Indian higher education system. Innovations in higher education system is very insignificant. No wonder, in spite of the large number of higher education institutions in the country, we do not figure in the world class institutions by the expert ranking agencies. Our higher education system needs reforms in many aspects:

- The enrolment rates have to be significantly improved to reach the status of a developed nation (30-50%).
- Financial resources have to be enhanced for the large number of state establishments.
- Teacher quality needs to be enhanced through multiple training options.
- Appropriate vocational education programmes relevant to the needs of the society have to be identified and implemented to enhance employability of graduates.
- Utilise resources optimally for academic growth and excellence.
- Re-build existing institutions to make them more productive enterprises with reference to a student's academic growth and career advancement.
- Better utilisation of ICT infrastructure in academics and administration.
- Curriculum to meet the global challenges through the competencies and skills developed among the students.

Employers often feel that graduates are not employable. The educational system of the country need to produce knowledge workers who are competitive and innovative. Therefore, it is easy to guess that most of the current higher education institutions which focus on the attainment of a discrete body of specialist knowledge is no longer relevant. Employers now want their workforce to be flexible and innovative, demanding them to be capable of learning new skill and acquire relevant knowledge as the need arises. Educational institutions therefore, must establish a Research Consultancy Centres involving faculty, professionals, students and industry, where work on few technologies and discovery is facilitated. The focus has to be on commercially viable research and consultancy.

The Higher education system needs to increasingly focus on the importance of quality assessment, assurance and enhancement. The changes in higher education should be much more accountable to all their stakeholders, not least to the students.

- Higher education institutions should undergo a continuous need assessment. They should assess the major requirements of stakeholders of the higher education system, in order to sense their changing needs, expectations and perceptions of the forces driving the change. They have to have an effective management information system to enable them to make quick and relevant decisions.
- Students are encouraged to be active participants in the learning process. Therefore, there should be more student focus in the curriculum, curriculum transaction and other management aspects. Students need to develop critical reflective thinking skills, the ability to make one's own informed judgments in a world in which multiple educational outcomes like complex cognitive skills, ability to apply acquired · knowledge of complex life problems, appreciation of human differences, practical competence skills and a coherent integrated sense of identity, etc. exists.
- Promoting employability of graduates is a key. Work experience can be very valuable in helping students to obtain the right orientation. This would enhance the marketability of the educational programmes.
- Prospective students differ in terms of their financial capabilities. Therefore differential fee structure and availability of assistantship/scholarship/loan etc. should be very useful.
- The adoption of information technology both in academics and administration is a must. Information and communication technologies through the internet and satellite transmission have opened up avenues of development in educational delivery modes which should be engaged by all institutions.

- The role of the teacher will change to a facilitator. Only a facilitator would be able to improve a student's receptivity to knowledge, by influencing their perception of nature, limits, certainty and utility of knowledge.
- It will require an efficient and effective managerial system through programmes of human resource development. It will also need a very different decision making structure from the present bodies of the university. Hence, it will need a radical change in the structure and constitution of its management bodies, if decision-making becomes time bound and professionally oriented.
- The universities have to become manageable in size. Its span of control have to be reduced with more and more decentralisation. With decentralisation, autonomy of the colleges, and even departments of universities, will have to be promoted while ensuring accountability. This probably is the only way to make the system effective in all respects
- Various subsystems in the education system will have to synergize in a major cooperative effort to make our system innovative and competitive with the best in the world. New patterns of governance and leadership capable of responding to the changing scenario and emerging challenges have to be evolved.
- Since technology is transforming the work place, requiring greater technical skills for a growing number of jobs, there is a need to reorient the academic programmes to help them develop necessary skills and expertise to function effectively in a technologically enabled work place. It is important that the skills have economic value content beyond the specialized knowledge that it enjoys in their area of specialisation. (Varghese, 2014)

Functions of the Universities in the Changing World

Prevailing discourse, familiar since at least the 1990s, emphasizes the university's place as a paramount player in a global system increasingly driven by knowledge, information and ideas. We live in a time when knowledge is ever more vital to our societies and economies, in a world of rapidly circulating capital and people and of revolutionary communication technologies. Knowledge is replacing other resources as the main driver of economic growth, and education has increasingly become the foundation for individual prosperity and social mobility. Higher education generates broader economic growth as well as individual success. (Faust, 2010). Functions of the universities in the changing world are:

- To seek and cultivate new knowledge, to engage 'vigorously and fearlessly in the pursuit of truth and to interpret old knowledge and beliefs in the light of new needs and discoveries;
- To provide the right kind of leadership in all walks of life by helping the individuals develop their potential;
- To provide society with competent men and women trained in all professions who, as cultivated individuals, are inclined with a sense of social purpose;
- To strive to promote equality and social justice and to reduce social and cultural differences through diffusion of education;
- To foster in the teachers and students in the society generally, the attitudes and values needed for developing the "good life" in individuals and society;
- To bring the universities closer to the community through extension of knowledge and its implications for problem-solving.

Vision of India on Higher Education

Education aims at liberation - liberation from bondage and ignorance, backwardness and gravitational pulls of the lower human nature. Education, being an evolutionary force that enables both the individual and the collectively to evolve various faculties and to integrate them by the superior intellectual, ethical, aesthetic and spiritual powers. Education should be so designed as to become a powerful carrier of the best of the heritage and it should, therefore, aim at transmitting to the new generations the lessons of the accumulated experiences of the past for further progress in the present and the future.

Universities and Contemporary Change

The 1980s and then 1990s have witnessed rapid changes in the domain of higher education. Internationalization and globalization today are high on the agendas of governments and higher education institutions. Universities are at present engaging in enrolling international students, becoming partners in inter-institutional schemes, and pushing forward in the drive towards globalization. Students, academic staff and curricula are transferred and exchanged between institutions. Accreditation agencies ensure promptness in accrediting arming experiences and governments append their signatures to cooperative projects. Universities must themselves change, as otherwise their future will be defined by political and business elites. The task facing people in higher education is to think beyond the constraints of conventional wisdom. For example, it is being envisaged that traditional degree programmes will increasingly be replaced by continuing education or lifelong learning than research. Teachers will become facilitators than the transmitters of knowledge. Different forms of knowledge generation to suit the diversified student population and different markets is likely to emerge. It is not only the developments of liberalization, privatization and globalization which will play a crucial role in setting the aims, role and functions of the HEIs in the near future.

Present Status of Indian Higher Education

Total number of Universities in India as on 30.09.2014	
State Universities	322
Deemed to be Universities	128
Central Universities	45
Private Universities	192
Total No. of Universities	687

Source: http://www.ugc.ac.in/oldpdf/alluniversity.pdf

Other institutions include 16000 colleges, including 1800 exclusive women's colleges. The emphasis in the tertiary level of education lies on science and technology. Indian educational institutions consisted of a large number of technology institutes. Distance learning is also a feature of the Indian higher education system. Some institutions of India, such as the IITs, have been globally acclaimed for their standard of UG education in engineering. Several other institutes of fundamental research are acclaimed for their standard of research in basic sciences and mathematics. However, India has failed to produce world class universities both in the private sector or the public sector. The Number of graduates coming out of technical colleges increased to over 700,000 in 2011 from 550,000 in the financial year 2010. However, 75% of technical graduates and more than 85% of general graduates are unemployable. From the first Five Year Plan onwards India's emphasis was to develop a pool of scientifically inclined manpower.

Higher Education in India - 12th Five Year Plan (2012-2017) and beyond

India has one of the largest Higher Education systems in the world, with 25.9 million students enrolled in more than 45,000 degree and diploma institutions in the country. The Government intends to achieve enrolment of 35.9 million students in higher education institutions, with a GER of 25.2%, by the end of the 12th Five Year Plan period through the co-existence of multiple types of institutions including research-centric, teaching and vocation-focused ones. The private sector can be expected to play an instrumental role for the same. (Jhingan, 2014) Private institutions now account for 64% of the total number of institutions and 59% of enrolment in the country, as compared to 43% and 33%, respectively, a decade ago. The Government has also given the required thrust to the sector in its 5 Year Plans. During the 11th Plan period (2007-2012), India achieved a GER of 17.9%, up from 12.3% at the beginning of the Plan period.

Indian Universities and their Tryst with Global Rankings

In April 2013, Times Higher Education released its first university rankings dedicated to the Asian Higher Education sector. Punjab University and IIT Kharagpur got 32nd and 45th ranks respectively in the same. Later this year 2014, the whole of Indian academia is celebrating the fact that two of Indian Universities ranked for the first time by the Times Higher Education (THE) has figured among the top 40. Indian Institute of Science (IISc) has been ranked 25, Indian Institute of Technology (IIT) Bombay at 37th place in the recently announced in the ranking of universities in BRICS and emerging economies 2015 by THE. However, when once compares India with other BRICS (Brazil, Russia, India, China and South Africa) countries, all the nations have representation among top 10 with India as the only exception. This is more so because after China among BRICS, India has the maximum number of Institutions ranked among the top 100, varsities from 22 countries emerging economies have been ranked.

China has continuously strengthened its position as the best among the emerging economies and has retained the top two positions (Peking University followed by Tsinghua University) in the rankings, and claims a total of 27 top-100 institutions, up from 23 last year. Fudan University follows Peking and Tsinghua, taking ninth place, while University of Science and Technology of China loses its top-10 position, moving into joint 11th place. Taiwan is the next best represented country with 19 universities in the top-100 list, but this compares with 21 institutions last year.

Last year in the inaugural edition of Ranking, India had 10 universities among the top 100, while this year it has improved slightly and has gone up to 11. The best debut performer has been the Indian Institute of Science (IISc) at 25, which is followed by another debutant IIT Bombay at 37, the other two universities among top 40 are IIT Roorkee and Panjab University, Chandigarh at 38 and 39 respectively. Other institutions among top 100 are IIT Kharagpur at 43, which was ranked 30 last year, IIT Delhi has also lost its previous years rank of 37 and has slipped to 56, Jawaharlal Nehru University (JNU), IIT Kanpur and Aligarh Muslim University (AMU) all three have also lost their last year's rank and has gone down from 57 to 71, 34 to 74, 50 to 78, respectively. IIT Madras is the only university from India that has improved upon its last year's rank, it has moved three positions, it is now at 44 against last year's 47. The situation is worst for IIT Guwahati which has slipped from 46 last year to 98 this year.

Phil Baty, editor of the *Times Higher Education Rankings* talking about Indian universities said "India is starting to show its potential in these rankings, increasing its overall representation in this new top-100 list to 11, from 10 last year. Only China and Taiwan have more top-100 institutions than India, which remains ahead of Russia and Brazil among the giant developing economies. But this improved showing is partly due to the fact that more Indian institutions have recognised the benefits of being part of the rankings process, and more are sharing their data with Times Higher Education." The good news is that by engaging with the global rankings and sharing performance data to benchmark themselves against the tough global standards set by THE, India's leading institutions have shown a hunger for further development and for sharing best practice. (India Education Review, 2014)

The Times Higher Education (THE) World University Rankings 2014-2015 list the best global universities and are the only international university performance tables to judge world class universities across all of their core missions - teaching, research, knowledge transfer and international outlook. The top universities rankings employ 13 carefully calibrated performance indicators to provide the most comprehensive and balanced comparisons available, which are trusted by students, academics, university leaders, industry and governments. World University Rankings 2014-2015 is a sophisticated exercise in information-gathering and analysis. The Times Higher Education World University Rankings are the only global university performance tables to judge research-led universities across all their core missions - teaching, research, knowledge transfer and international outlook. In the THE World University Rankings 2014-2015 Indian Institute of Science Bangalore and Punjab University go the 276th rank. The THE World University Rankings employ 13 carefully calibrated performance indicators to provide the most comprehensive and balanced comparisons, which are trusted by students, academics, university leaders, industry and governments. The methodology for the 2014-2015 World University Rankings is identical to that used since 2011-2012, offering a year-on-year comparison based on true performance rather than methodological change. The 13 performance indicators of THE ranking are grouped into five areas:

1. Teaching: the learning environment (worth 30 per cent of the overall ranking score);
2. Research: volume, income and reputation (worth 30 per cent);
3. Citations: research influence (worth 30 per cent);
4. Industry income: innovation (worth 2.5 per cent);
5. International outlook: staff, students and research (worth 7.5 per cent).

Conclusion

India's higher education system can be expected to be better aligned to industry and global practices, and be more transparent and inclusive by the end of Twelfth Plan period, provided the Government is able to create an enabling regulatory environment and put in place robust implementation, monitoring and quality assurance mechanisms. India has seen a consistently high rate of economic growth in the recent years. India now become a major player in the global knowledge economy. Skill-based activities have made significant contribution to this growth. Such activities depend on the large pool of qualified manpower that is fed by its large higher education system. It is now widely accepted that higher education has been critical to India's emergence in the global knowledge economy. India faces enormous social challenges as well as opportunities for rapid development in the new millennium. Our unprecedented recent economic growth, the values of knowledge and education shared by a 1.26 billion diverse people, and the investments made over the last half century, all point to India's potential future as a knowledge economy with high level man/women power in the science and technology driven global village. The investment made in education given us a strong knowledge base in many fields contributed significantly to economic development, social progress and political democracy in independent India. Higher Education in India is one of the most developed in the entire world. The growth of the Indian economy in the recent past and the compulsion to sustain it is also forcing the Indian government to accelerate the process of developing all the branches of the Indian education system.

REFERENCES

1. Agarwal, P. (2009). *Indian Higher Education: Envisioning the Future*. India: Sage retrieved on 18th April 2015 from http://www.indianhighereducation.org/introduction.html
2. Association of Indian Universities (1993) *Excellence in Achieving Social Relevance in Higher Education*, New Delhi: AIU
3. Association of Indian Universities (1998). *Accountability and Autonomy in Higher Education*, New Delhi: AIU
4. Association of Indian Universities (2003). *Privatization of Higher Education*, New Delhi: AIU
5. Government of India (1949). *Report of the Education Commission, 1964-66*. New Delhi: Ministry of Education.
6. Government of India (1949). *Report of the University Education Commission, 1948-49*). New Delhi: Ministry of Education.
7. *Indian Universities and their Tryst with Global Rankings*. retrieved on 12th March 2015 from http://www.indiaeducationreview.com/features/indian-universities-and-their-tryst-global-rankings/18397
8. Jhingan, A. (2014). *Higher Education in India - Twelfth Five Year Plan (2012–2017) and beyond*. retrieved on 9th November 2014 from http://www.ey.com/ IN/en/ Industries/ India-sectors/ Education/Higher-Education-in-India—Twelfth-Five-Year-Plan–2012-2017–and-beyond
9. Mehta, A.C. (1998). *Education for All in India - Enrolment Projections*. New Delhi: NIEPA & Vikas Publishing House.
10. MHRD. (2003). *Education in India* (Vol. I & Vol. II), 1995-96. New Delhi, Government of India.

11. MHRD. (2004). *Selected Educational Statistics: 2002-03*. New Delhi, Government of India.

12. Narayan, J. (2005). *Reforming Higher Education in India*, Hyderabad: Foundation for Democratic Reforms/Lok Satta. Retrieved on 5th January 2015 from http: //www.loksatta.org/cms /documents /advocacy /highedu.pdf

13. Reuters, T. (Ed.). World University Rankings 2014-15. Retrieved June 21, 2015, from https://www.timeshighereducation.co.uk/world-university-rankings/2015/world-ranking#/

14. Sam Pitroda, (2009). *National Knowledge Commission Report*. New Delhi: MHRD

15. *The Role of the University in a Changing World*. (2010, June 30). Retrieved December 17, 2014, from http://www.harvard.edu/president/speech/2010/role-university-changing-world

16. Varghese, M.A. (2015). *Indian Higher Education at a Crossroad*, Retrieved June 21, 2015, from http://www.dnaindia.com/academy/report-indian-higher-education-at-a-crossroad-2021059

19 Higher Education in the Changing Indian Context

Introduction

Education is vital to the human resources development and empowerment in the stages of growth of a nation. Education plays a major role in imparting knowledge, values, and developing skills and, in the process, increase the growth and productivity of the country. While the State is committed to providing education and certain facilities/subsidies for education, given the higher cost involved in the establishment of education institutes. The principal objective of education is the development of an individual in total. Education in India, has reached a remarkable height, since independence. Successive Indian governments have had to address a number of key challenges with regard to education policy throughout these days. India's huge pool of young people might be considered its biggest strength. Unfortunately, India is far from having its act together when it comes to figuring out how to educate these young people. Government data suggests that only one out of every seven children born in India goes to college. India suffers quantity as well as a quality challenge in higher education.

After India became free and set about the task of reorienting its educational system to suit the needs and aspirations of an independent nation committed to Democracy, Secularism and Socialism, intensive and widespread discussions have taken place on the aims and purposes of its higher education. These discussions have involved all concerned with higher education, teachers, students, parents, educationists and leaders in the community. Their considered views have found expression in important national documents like reports of Commissions and Committees and statements of National Policies.

Ministry of Education was appointed a commission under the chairmanship of Dr. Sarvepally Radhakrishnan to report on Indian university education. Dr. Radhakrishnan recognizes that *"If India is to confront the confusion our times, she must turn for guidance not to those who are lost to the exigencies of the passing hour but to her men of letters and men of science, to her poets and artists to her discoverers and inventors. These intellectual pioneers of civilization are to be found and trained in the universities, which are the sanctuaries of the minor life of the nation"*.

The University is the place where the right kind of leadership in all walks of life is developed. Gifted youths in different pursuits of excellence are identified. The University then helps in inculcation of physical fitness, the development of the powers of the mind, cultivation of the right interests, attitudes and promotion of moral and intellectual values. In the modem days, the University should promote a rational outlook and nurture scientific temper among the youth. It should wipe out dogmatism, fundamentalism and prejudices from the minds of the youth. On the other hand, it should develop right kind of temperament and ability to judge between right and wrong, good and evil.

The report of the Education Commission (1964-66) says about the universities that they are the dwelling places of ideas and idealism, and expect high standards of conduct and integrity from all their members. Theirs is the pursuit of truth and excellence in all its diversity a pursuit which needs, above all, courage and fearlessness. *"Great universities and timid people go ill together"*; It is instructive to study what kind of mind was to be cultivated in the universities according to the Education Commission. Dealing with the special responsibilities of the universities the Commission says: "...the universities must learn to encourage individuality, variety and dissent within a climate of tolerance".

The Education Commission (1964-1966) set out the following functions of the Universities in the modern world:

- To seek and cultivate new knowledge, to engage 'vigorously and fearlessly in the pursuit of truth and to interpret old knowledge and beliefs in the light of new needs and discoveries;
- To provide the right kind of leadership in all walks of life by helping the individuals develop their potential;
- To provide society with competent men and women trained in all professions who, as cultivated individuals, are inclined with a sense of social purpose;
- To strive to promote equality and social justice and to reduce social and cultural differences through diffusion of education;
- To foster in the teachers and students in the society generally, the attitudes and values needed for developing the "good life" in individuals and society;

- To bring the universities closer to the community through extension of knowledge and its implications for problem-solving.

Higher education, according to the NPE 1986, provides people with an opportunity to reflect on the critical social, economic, cultural, moral and spiritual issues facing humanity. It contributes to national development through dissemination of specialized knowledge and skills. It is, therefore, a crucial factor for survival. Being at the apex of the educational pyramid, it has also a key role in producing teachers for the education system. In the context of the unprecedented explosion of knowledge, higher education had to become dynamic as never before, constantly entering uncharted areas, and it proposed that the large number of universities and colleges in the country needed improvement and that the main emphasis in the immediate future should be on their consolidation and expansion (NPE, 1986).

The country paper (Government of India) articulating the vision of India on higher education in 1998 reflected the following views:

- Education aims at liberation - liberation from bondage and ignorance, backwardness and gravitational pulls of the lower human nature;
- Education, being an evolutionary force that enables both the individual and the collectively to evolve various faculties and to integrate them by the superior intellectual, ethical, aesthetic and spiritual powers, should aim at developing a new type of humanity highly humane, cultured and integrated;
- Education should be so designed as to become a powerful carrier of the best of the heritage and it should, therefore, aim at transmitting to the new generations the lessons of the accumulated experiences of the past for further progress in the present and the future.

Universities and Contemporary Change

The 1980s and then 1990s have witnessed rapid changes in the domain of higher education. Internationalization and globalization today are high on the agendas of governments and universities. The global economy is only now beginning to bear upon the international role of higher education. Universities are at present engaging in enrolling international students, becoming partners in inter-institutional schemes, and pushing forward in the drive towards globalization, students, academic staff and curricula are transferred and exchanged between institutions, accreditation agencies ensure promptness in accrediting arming experiences and governments append their signatures to cooperative projects in higher education. Universities, in general, must take the initiative in defining radically different arrangements for their future if only for their own good: Universities must themselves change, as otherwise their future will be defined by political and business elites.

The task facing people in higher education is to think beyond the constraints of conventional wisdom, if universities are to respond to the challenges and uncertainties of the new century, they must find fresh ways to do so against the backdrop of globalization and linking education to industry and the world of work, certain changes in the basic aims of universities seem in the offing. For example, it is being envisaged that traditional degree programmes will increasingly be replaced by continuing education or lifelong learning than research will take place, teachers will become facilitators than the main transmitters of bodies of knowledge, different forms of knowledge generation to suit the diversified student population and different markets is likely to emerge dong with varied mechanisms for dissemination and delivery of knowledge. Further it is not only the developments of globalization and liberalization which will play a crucial role in setting the aims, role and functions of the university in the near future. The limits on what universities can achieve are also set by the societies in which they function. In this context it is being felt that "universities, despite all the changes they have made, have not responded and are also responding, with sufficient speed or at an appropriate level, to the technological, economic, social and demographic changes of the past twenty years" (Coffield & Williamson, 1997). Further, "it is not enough for universities to reform themselves. They must seek to engage in a deranging and critical dialogue within society to secure the conditions of both the future growth and sustainable development of both".

Present Status of Indian Higher Education

India's higher education system is the third largest in the world, after China and the United States. The main governing body at the tertiary level is the University Grants Commission (India), which enforces its standards, advises the government, and helps coordinate between the center and the state. In future, India will be one of the largest education hubs.

Some institutions of India, such as the Indian Institutes of Technology (IITs), have been globally acclaimed for their standard of undergraduate education in engineering. Several other institutes of fundamental research such as Tata Institute of Fundamental Research (TIFR), Harishchandra Research Institute (HRI), are acclaimed for their standard of research in basic sciences and mathematics. However, India has failed to produce world class universities both in the private sector or the public sector. Besides top rated universities which provide highly competitive world class education to their pupils, India is also home to many universities which have been founded with the sole objective of making easy money.

Regulatory authorities like UGC and AICTE have been trying very hard to extirpate the menace of private universities which are running courses without any affiliation or recognition. Many private colleges and universities do not fulfill the required criterion by the Government and central bodies (UGC, AICTE, MCI, BCI etc). Quality assurance mechanism has failed to stop misrepresentations and malpractices in higher education. At the same time regulatory bodies have been accused of corruption, specifically in the case of deemed-universities. In this context of lack of solid quality assurance mechanism, institutions need to step-up and set higher standards of self-regulation.

Foreign Universities Bill (2010), which is supposed to facilitate entry of foreign universities to establish campuses in India. One of the approaches to make internationalization of Indian higher education effective is to develop a coherent and comprehensive policy which aims at infusing excellence, bringing institutional diversity and aids in capacity building. In April 2013, Times Higher Education released its first university rankings dedicated to the Asian higher education sector. The Asia University Rankings judge world class universities across all of their core missions - teaching, research, knowledge transfer and international outlook, and provide the positions of top 100 Asian tertiary institutes. Punjab University and Indian Institute of Technology, Kharagpur got 32nd and 45th ranks respectively. The number of graduates coming out of technical colleges increased to over 700,000 in 2011 from 550,000 in the financial year (FY) 2010 However, 75% of technical graduates and more than 85% of general graduates are unemployable by India's high-growth global industries, including information technology and call centers. From the first Five Year Plan onwards India's emphasis was to develop a pool of scientifically inclined manpower. The UGC has Inter-University Centers (IUCs) at a number of locations throughout India to promote common research. Central Universities such as Banaras Hindu University, Jamia Millia Islamia, Delhi University etc. are too pioneers of tertiary education in the country. In addition to above institutes, efforts towards the enhancement of technical education are supplemented by a number of recognized Professional institutions.

Governing Goals of Higher Education

It is necessary to recognized that the present approach towards higher education is governed by the National policy on Education 1986 (NPE 1986) and Programme of Action 1992. The University Education Commission of 1948-49 and the Education Commission 1964-66, are the two landmark reports in fact laid down the basic framework for the NPE.

While articulating goals for development of higher education, University Education Commission put it in following words; *"The most important and urgent reform needed in education is to transform it, to endeavor to relate it to the life, needs and aspirations of the people and thereby make it the powerful instrument of social, economic and cultural transformation necessary for the realization of the national goals. For this purpose, education should be developed so as to increase productivity, achieve social and national integration, accelerate the process of modernization and cultivate social, moral and spiritual values."* The NPE 1986 translate this vision in goals for higher education which include *Greater Access, Equal access (or equity), Quality and excellence, Relevance and promotion of social Values.*

Higher Education in India - Twelfth Five Year Plan (2012-2017) and beyond

India has one of the largest higher education systems in the world, with 25.9 million students enrolled in more than 45,000 degree and diploma institutions in the country. It has witnessed particularly high growth in the last decade, with enrollment of students increasing. Moreover, the Government intends to achieve enrollment of 35.9 million students in higher education institutions, with a GER of 25.2%, by the end of the Twelfth Five Year Plan period through the co-existence of multiple types of institutions including research-centric, teaching and vocation-focused ones. The private sector can be expected to play an instrumental role in the achievement of these outcomes through the creation of knowledge networks, research and innovation centers, corporate-backed institutions, and support for faculty development (Jhingan, 2014). With the objectives and proposals of the Plan as the basis, the report mentions that the private sector has played an instrumental role in the growth of the sector. Private institutions now account for 64% of the total number of institutions and 59% of enrollment in the country, as compared to 43% and 33%, respectively, a decade ago. The Government has also given the required thrust to the sector in its Five Year Plans. During the Eleventh Plan period (2007-2012), India achieved a Gross Enrollment Ratio (GER) of 17.9%, up from 12.3% at the beginning of the Plan period. India's higher education system faces challenges on three fronts:

1. **Expansion:**
   - India's GER of16% was much below the world average of 27%, as well as that of other emerging countries such as China (26%) and Brazil (36%) in 2010.
2. **Excellence:**
   - Faculty shortage - there is 40% and 35% shortage of faculty in state and central universities, respectively.
   - Accredited institutions - 62% of universities and 90% of colleges were average or below average in 2010, on the basis of their NAAC accreditation.

- Low citation impact - India's relative citation impact is half the world average.

3. **Equity:** There is wide disparity in the GER of higher education across states and the Gross Attendance Ratio (GAR) in urban and rural areas, and gender- and community-wise
   - Inter-state disparity - 47.9% in Delhi vs. 9% in Assam.
   - Urban-rural divide - 30% in urban areas vs. 11.1% in rural areas.
   - Differences across communities - 14.8% for OBCs, 11.6% for SCs, 7.7% for STs and 9.6% for Muslims.
   - Gender disparity - 15.2% for females vs. 19% for males.

Next steps:

- **Merit-based student financing:** This should ensure admissions to meritorious students independent of financial background.
- **Internationalization of education:** This would entail aligning different aspects of education (curriculum, faculty, etc) to international standards.
- **Enabling a research environment:** This would involve creating adequate means of research funding and practical application of research.
- **High quality faculty:** The need of the hour is to create a conducive environment and provide incentives to attract and retain high quality faculty.
- **Improved technology for education delivery:** Leveraging technology for enhancing the teaching-learning experience will ensure better outcomes.
- **Employability:** Making education-industry relevant and practical would be the right way to ensure a highly employable talent pool.

India's higher education system can be expected to be better aligned to industry and global practices, and be more transparent and inclusive by the end of Twelfth Plan period, provided the Government is able to create an enabling regulatory environment and put in place robust implementation, monitoring and quality assurance mechanisms.

Conclusion

India has seen a consistently high rate of economic growth in the recent years. India now become a major player in the global knowledge economy. Skill-based activities have made significant contribution to this growth. Such activities depend on the large pool of qualified manpower that is fed by its large higher education system. It is now widely accepted that higher education has been critical to India's emergence in the global knowledge economy. India faces enormous social challenges as well as opportunities for rapid development in the new millennium. Our unprecedented recent economic growth, the values of knowledge and education shared by a 1.26 billion diverse people, and the investments made over the last half century, all point to India's potential future as a knowledge economy with high level man/women power in the science and technology driven global village. The investment made in education given us a strong knowledge base in many fields contributed significantly to economic development, social progress and political democracy in independent India. Higher Education in India is one of the most developed in the entire world. The growth of the Indian economy in the recent past and the compulsion to sustain it is also forcing the Indian government to accelerate the process of developing all the branches of the Indian education system.

REFERENCES

1. Agarwal, P. (2009). *Indian Higher Education: Envisioning the Future*. India: Sage retrieved from http://www.indianhighereducation.org/introduction.html
2. Association of Indian Universities (1993) *Excellence in Achieving Social Relevance in Higher Education*, New Delhi: AIU.
3. Association of Indian Universities (1998) *Accountability and Autonomy in Higher Education*, New Delhi: AIU.
4. Association of Indian Universities (2003) *Privatization of Higher Education*, New Delhi: AIU.
5. http://en.wikipedia.org/wiki/Times_Higher_Education_World_University_Rankings
6. http://mhrd.gov.in/sites/upload_files/mhrd/files/YPC-Report_0.pdf
7. http://www.educationforallinindia.com/page80.html
8. http://www.wg.aegee.org/ewg/higheredu.htm
9. Jhingan, A. (2014). *Higher Education in India - Twelfth Five Year Plan (2012–2017) and beyond*. retrieved on 9th November 2014 from http://www.ey.com/ IN/en/ Industries/India-sectors/ Education/Higher-Education-in-India–Twelfth-Five-Year-Plan–2012-2017–and-beyond
10. Mehta, A.C. (1998) *Education for All in India - Enrolment Projections*. New Delhi: NIEPA & Vikas Publishing House.
11. MHRD. (2003). *Education in India* (Vol. I & Vol. II), 1995-96. New Delhi, Government of India.
12. MHRD. (2004). *Selected Educational Statistics: 2002-03*. New Delhi, Government of India.
13. Ministry of Education, Government of India (1949) *Report of the Education Commission, 1964-66* New Delhi.
14. Ministry of Education, Government of India (1949) *Report of the University Education Commission, 1948-49*). New Delhi.
15. Narayan, J (2005) *Reforming Higher Education in India,* Hyderabad: Foundation for Democratic Reforms/Lok Satta. Retrived from http: //www.loksatta.org/cms/ documents/advocacy/highedu.pdf
16. Sam Pitroda, *National Knowledge Commission Report*, New Delhi: MHRD

Index

U

V

W

❑ ❑ ❑ ❑ ❑